Visual QuickStart Guide

Microsoft Works 2.0
for Windows

Suzie Wynn Jones

Webster & Associates

Peachpit Press

Microsoft Works for Windows Visual QuickStart Guide
Suzie Wynn Jones

Peachpit Press, Inc.
2414 Sixth Street
Berkeley, CA 94710

First edition published 1992

ISBN: 0-938151-99-1

Printed and bound in the United States of America

Why a Visual QuickStart?

Virtually no one actually reads computer books; rather, people typically refer to them. This series of **Visual QuickStart Guides** has made that reference easier thanks to a new approach to learning computer applications.

While conventional computer books lean towards providing extensive textual explanations, a **Visual QuickStart Guide** takes a far more visual approach—pictures literally show you what to do, and text is limited to clear, concise commentary. Learning becomes easier, because a **Visual QuickStart Guide** familiarizes you with the look and feel of your software. Learning also becomes faster, since there are no long-winded passages to comb through.

It's a new approach to computer learning, but it's also solidly based on experience: Webster & Associates have logged thousands of hours of classroom computer training, and have authored several books on desktop publishing topics.

Chapter 1 provides a general introduction to Microsoft Works for Windows and discusses the screen components.

Chapters 2 through **6** graphically overview the major Microsoft Works for Windows features; these chapters are easy to reference and their extensive use of screen shots helps you quickly understand how to operate Works' tools.

Appendix A displays all the major dialog boxes and shows how to access them.

Acknowledgments

This book was developed with the assistance of many of the staff at Webster & Associates. The author would like to thank Roger Stott for initial research, Tony Webster for technical checking and proofreading, and Jenny Hamilton for editing.

We would also like to thank the people "behind the scenes" for their invaluable technical expertise. These people include Paul Webster, David Webster, Wayne Clark, and Mike King.

Contents

WORKS FOR WINDOWS

INTRODUCTION

Microsoft Works is an easy-to-use, yet powerful collection of software applications or "tools." Works for Windows contains three tools—a word processor, a spreadsheet, and a database.

A package, such as Works, that contains more than one type of software application is referred to as an *integrated package*. Using an integrated product such as Works offers users two major advantages:

1. The tools operate uniformly, making an integrated package quick and easy to learn; many processes are identical in each tool.
2. The word processor, spreadsheet, and database are designed to work together, making it easy to transport and link data between tools.

WORD PROCESSOR

Figure 1. The Word Processor is used for writing letters, memos, and business proposals or essays. Text is typed directly onto the screen. If you make a mistake, you can easily edit the text without having to retype the document.

You can change the appearance of text by using different fonts, such as Palatino, Times and Helvetica, and different attributes, such as boldfaces, italics or underlining.

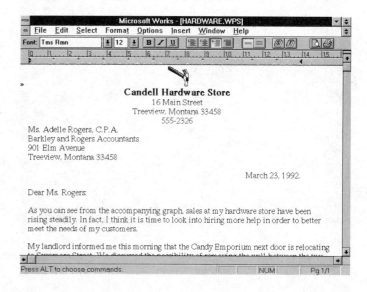

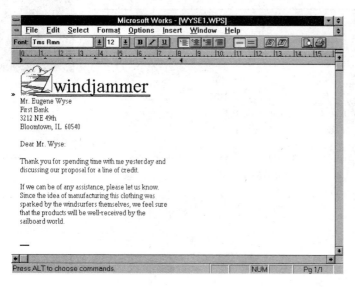

Figure 2. Graphics can be added to your document through Microsoft Draw, which is part of the Word Processor. Using the drawing package, you can create graphics of your own and add clip art included with MS Draw to give your document a more professional look and feel.

SPREADSHEET

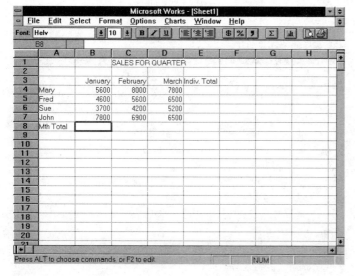

Figure 3. The Spreadsheet is an electronic piece of paper divided into columns and rows. It is generally used for preparing, analyzing, and presenting financial information.

You can enter text and numerical data into the Spreadsheet. These can be added across a row or down a column—whichever is most suitable for your spreadsheet.

Figure 4. Calculating ability is added by including formulas or mathematical functions to a spreadsheet. Basic formulas, such as adding and subtracting cell entries, can be added as well as mathematical functions. These built-in mathematical functions make entering complex formulas much simpler.

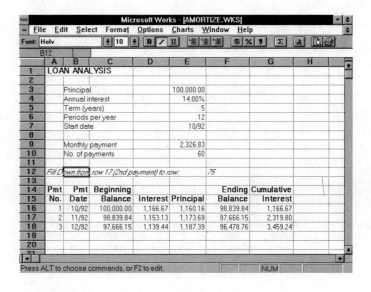

Figure 5. The appearance of a spreadsheet can be improved in many ways. A number of formatting options are available—for example, you can change or add borders to a spreadsheet.

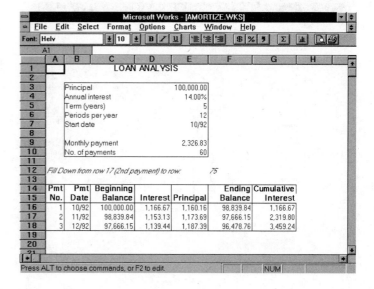

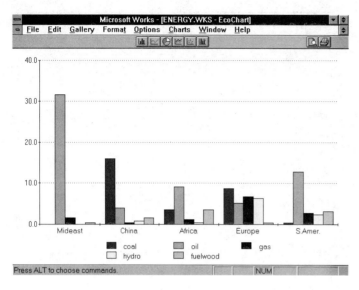

Figure 6. Information in a spreadsheet can be used to display a chart. A chart presents selected data in the spreadsheet in a graphical form. Most people find charts a much quicker and easier way to interpret figures.

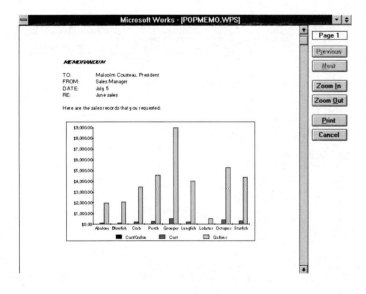

Figure 7. The chart can be imported into a word processor document and printed onto paper or overhead transparencies. The latter are useful for presentations.

DATABASE

Figure 8. A database is a collection of information organized in a logical way. You can use the database to make your own electronic filing system.

Databases are perfect for organizing client records, mailing lists, or inventories. Once created, up to 32,000 records in a Works database can be manipulated by your computer—in infinitely less time than you could do it manually.

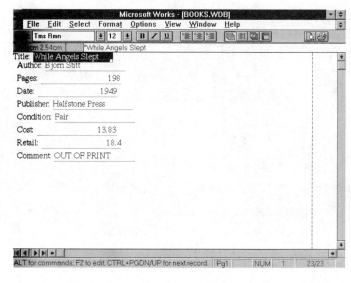

Figure 9. Your database can be viewed in two ways: *List* or *Form* view. In Figure 8, the database is in Form view—which displays only one record at a time. Figure 9 displays the data in List view—where many records in the database can be viewed simultaneously.

You can manipulate your database by sorting records into a specified order or searching for records that fit defined criteria.

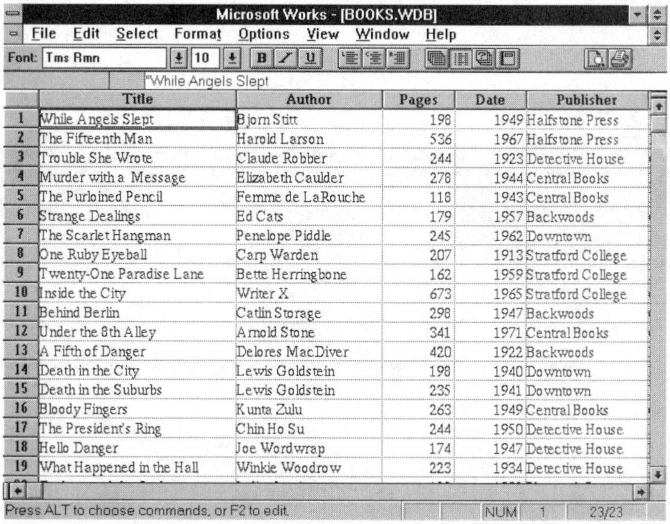

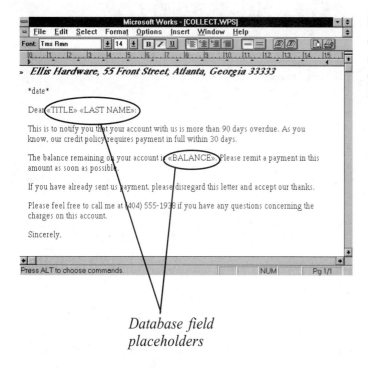

*Database field
placeholders*

Figure 10. Database information can be used in conjunction with a word processor document to create mailing labels, inventory lists, or form letters.

WORKSWIZARDS

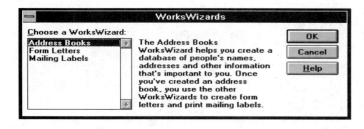

Figure 11. WorksWizards are a set of automated templates leading you through complex tasks. They can help you create an address book, form letters, and mailing labels.

Figure 12. Each WorksWizard consists of a series of screen displays that instruct you on how to complete each step of the task. When you have completed one step, you move into the next part of the activity by clicking on *Next* to continue.

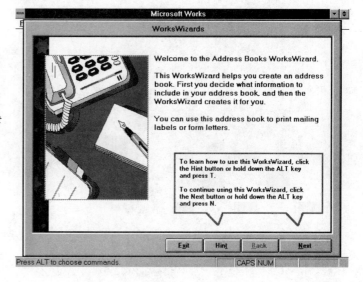

COMMON FEATURES 2

INTRODUCTION

Works has a number of common features that enable you to learn and use the product very efficiently and very quickly. Works is an easy product to learn for two main reasons:

1. It operates under Microsoft Windows and therefore uses a screen layout that is common to many other Windows applications. When you use Windows products, you can take advantage of the fact that tasks such as text editing, printing, and file handling follow similar procedures, so that moving from one Windows product to another is not difficult.

2. The Works for Windows menus and toolbars used in each of the tools are very similar. In many cases, the commands are identical. Where there are new commands to the menu structure, the overall appearance and "feel" of the application remains the same.

STARTING WORKS

Figure 1. When first installed, a *Welcome to Microsoft Works* dialog box appears on the screen. It offers three options:
- A guided tour of Works
- To start Works immediately
- To skip the welcome screen

Choosing the last option ensures that the *Welcome* dialog box will no longer appear on your screen whenever you start Works again.

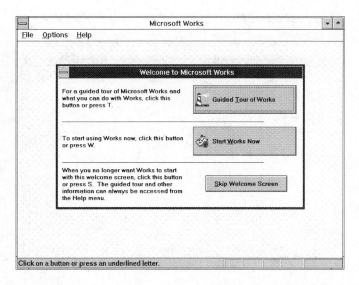

Figure 2. When Works for Windows is opened, a *Startup* dialog box usually appears in the middle of the screen as shown. When the *Startup* dialog box appears, you click on the button of the tool you want to activate. Alternatively, press the underlined letter corresponding to the required tool.

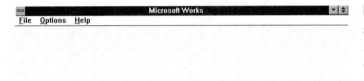

Figure 3. If no *Startup* dialog box appears, don't worry! You can make it appear by double-clicking anywhere in the blank screen.

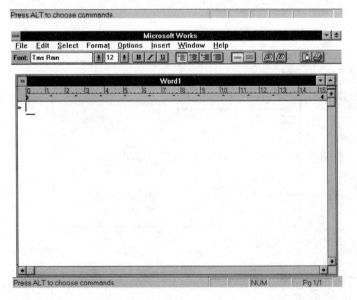

Figure 4. If you choose to open the Word Processor—by clicking on the Word Processor button or pressing "W" on the keyboard—the Word Processor will start, opening a blank document screen.

THE WORKS SCREEN

Each of the Works tools uses a similar screen layout. The components of the screens are used to create databases, spreadsheets, and written documents. Although the screen for each tool is unique in many ways, it also uses a number of common elements.

This section looks at those common features of the Works screen.

Figure 5. The screen that appears when you first start Works in any application shows you that there are in fact two windows open on the screen at the same time:

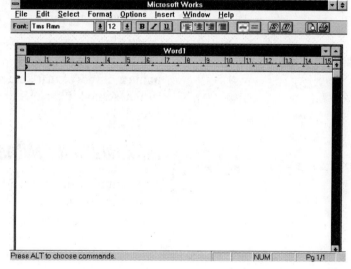

- An application window

- A document window

The application window contains the Works program and cannot be closed without closing Works completely.

The document window contains the file with which you are working. It could be a new document from any of the tools or a file which you have worked on previously. You can have a number of document windows (up to eight) open in Works simultaneously.

TITLE BAR

Figure 6. At the top of each window is a *Title Bar*. (On color screens Title Bars are usually a blue color.) The top Title Bar displays the program name of the program that is running in this application window—*Microsoft Works.*

The document window Title Bar contains the name of the file that is open in that window. If the document has been saved, the file name appears in the Title Bar.

If the file has not yet been saved, Works gives the document a temporary name according to the tool being used and the number of files of that kind that have been opened in the current session. Examples of such file names are titled Word1, Sheet1, Data1, etc.

MAXIMIZE AND MINIMIZE BUTTONS

The buttons at the right end of each Title Bar are used to enlarge and shrink the window. There are two options: *Maximize* and *Minimize.*

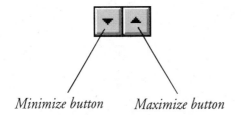

Minimize button   Maximize button

Figure 7. The arrowhead pointing down is the Minimize button. Clicking on this button will minimize the window so it appears as an icon in the bottom left of the screen. You can restore the icon to a window by double-clicking on it.

The arrowhead pointing up is the Maximize button. Using this button expands the window to fit the entire screen.

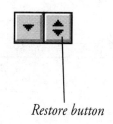

Restore button

Figure 8. When a screen is maximized, the Maximize button changes to a double arrowhead. This is called the *Restore* button; when clicked, it restores the window to its previous size before maximizing or minimizing.

To give you the largest possible screen area, maximize both the document and application windows before starting work. The shortcut for maximizing the screen is to double-click anywhere in the Title Bar.

CONTROL BAR

Control Bar

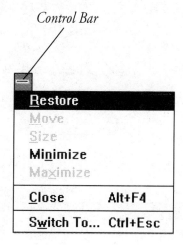

Figure 9. On the left side of the Title Bar is the *Control Bar.* Clicking on this box activates the Windows **Control** menu.

The options in the **Control** menu are a standard part of Windows, and contain such options as *Restore, Size, Move,* and *Switch To.* Each open window has its own **Control** menu, enabling you to manipulate each window individually.

MENU BAR

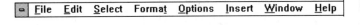

Figure 10. The *Menu Bar* appears just below the Title Bar. There are a number of menu options—such as **File**, **Edit**, and **Window**—each of which contains commands to perform specific tasks. In Works, many options on the Menu Bar are the same in each tool, although different options are available where necessary.

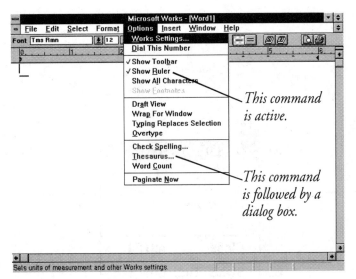

This command is active.

This command is followed by a dialog box.

Figure 11. When you click on a menu option, a list of commands will be displayed. A command followed by an ellipsis (...) indicates that a dialog box will be displayed. A check mark in front of an option indicates that it is selected and currently active.

Figure 12. When all files in Works are closed, only three menu options are displayed. These are **File**, **Options**, and **Help**.

SCROLL BARS

The Works screen contains two scroll bars. They are used to view unseen parts of your document. The slider button inside the scroll bars indicates the relative position within the whole document.

Figure 13. The vertical scroll bar, which is located on the right side of the screen, enables you to "scroll" up and down through your document.

The horizontal scroll bar, shown on the bottom of the screen, is used to move to the left and right in your document.

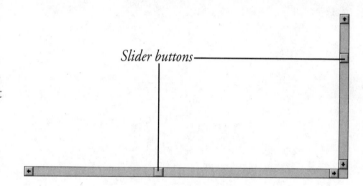

Slider buttons

The scroll bars can be used in a number of ways to move around your document:

- Click on the arrows at either end of the scroll bar to move in small steps.
- Click on the background area of the scroll bar to move more substantially.
- Drag the slider button up or down (or left or right) in the scroll bars to move in even larger steps—perhaps to move from one end of the document to the other.

TOOLBAR

Word Processor Toolbar

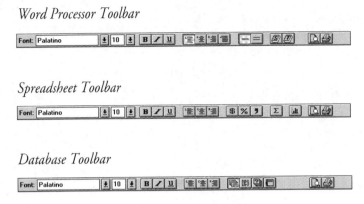

Spreadsheet Toolbar

Database Toolbar

Figure 14. The Toolbar is situated below the Menu Bar. It contains a number of shortcuts as alternatives to choosing commands from a menu. The Toolbar, therefore, makes Works much easier to use.

Most of the buttons on the Toolbar are identical in all tools. Additional buttons that perform specific tasks are placed on the Toolbars in the Word Processor, Spreadsheet, and Database.

The Toolbar is placed on the screen by default. If it is not displayed, open the **Options** menu and select the *Show Toolbar* command.

When a Toolbar button is active, it is slightly grayed on a monochrome screen; on a color screen, it is displayed in a different color to indicate that it is depressed. As the text cursor moves through the document, the active buttons change to give you information about the text at the cursor position.

Figure 15. Part of the Toolbar contains buttons and submenus that allow you to change the appearance of selected text. These do such things as change the font type and size, and can add bold, italic, and underline attributes to text. These buttons and submenus are common to each tool.

Figure 16. A submenu, such as *Font*, is opened by clicking on the down arrow to the right of the font name. When you click on this arrow, a list of fonts appears. The scroll bar next to this list indicates that there are more fonts available than can be shown.

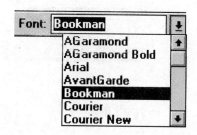

To move through the list of fonts, click on one of the scroll arrows and hold the mouse button down until the desired font comes into view. When it does appear, stop scrolling and click on the required font to apply it to the selected text.

Figure 17. The font size of selected text is altered in much the same way—by opening the *Size* submenu and scrolling through to find the required point size.

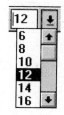

Figure 18. The alignment buttons are used to change the alignment (or justification) of a paragraph. A paragraph, cell, or field must be selected before any changes can be made.

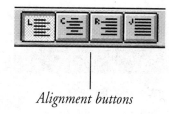

Alignment buttons

There are three choices in all tools—*Left*, *Center* and *Right*. The Word Processor provides an extra button, "J", which is designed to fully justify a paragraph.

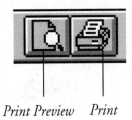

Print Preview   *Print*

Figure 19. The buttons on the right side of the Toolbar activate *Print* and *Print Preview* functions. These buttons are identified with icons; *Print Preview* displays a magnifying glass and *Print*, a printer image.

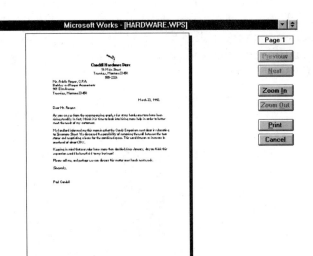

Figure 20. When you click on the *Print Preview* button, the document appears in a full-page outline—exactly the way it will print on a page.

You can use the *Print* button in this screen to print the document. Quit *Print Preview* by clicking on the *Cancel* button or by pressing the Esc key.

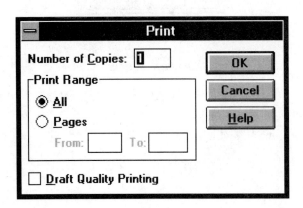

Figure 21. Select the *Print* icon on the Toolbar to go directly to the *Print* dialog box. The default settings here will print one copy of the complete document. If you don't want to print all the document, click on the *Pages* radio button, and then fill in the page range in the *From* and *To* boxes. When you are ready to print, press the Enter key or click on *OK*.

GETTING HELP

Figure 22. If you don't know how to perform a task in Works, help is close at hand! You can start Help by opening the **Help** menu. Works will give you a list of options when you activate Help from a document. Pressing the F1 key also activates Help.

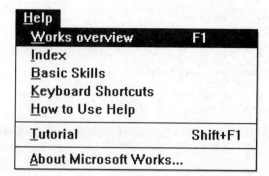

Help is designed to be easy to use and informative for the new user. If you need some assistance on getting started with the Help facility, you can choose the *How to Use Help* option to find out how the Help program itself works.

Many dialog boxes contain a *Help* button that can provide specific help information about the currently open dialog box.

In addition, if you are in a menu and activate Help using the F1 key, Works will display a Help window that is relevant to your current position in Works.

Figure 23. The buttons at the top of the Help screen are activated by either clicking on the required button or by pressing the Alt key and the underlined letter. For example, press Alt+I for Index. Works will display a complete list of all Help topics available.

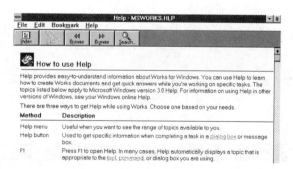

If you have opened a Help window and want to move back to the previous screen, click on the *Back* button. The *Browse* buttons allow you to read related topics.

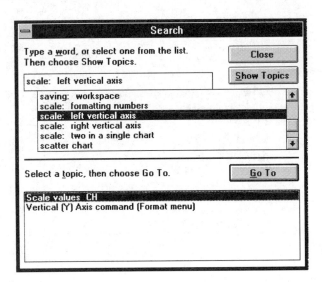

Figure 24. The *Search* button in the initial Help screen helps you to find the Help topic you want. When you click on the *Search* button, this dialog box is displayed. Enter the word or letters of the topic you need to find and click on the *Show Topics* button. (This dialog box may vary, depending on your version of Windows.)

Works scans every Help topic and displays those relevant in the *Topics Found* section. To see the topic, click on the most relevant topic in the list and then on the *Go To* button.

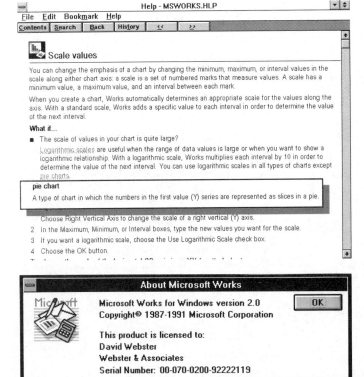

Figure 25. In a Help screen, underlined words in a different color contain an embedded definition. When the mouse pointer passes over a broken underlined word, the arrow pointer changes to a pointing finger. You can read the definition by either clicking or holding down the mouse button on the word (depending on your Windows version). To close the definition window, press Esc, or release or click on the mouse button.

Figure 26. *About Microsoft Works* (in the **Help** menu) lists information that may be useful if you are seeking technical support. It tells you the Works version number, the licensee of the software, and the serial number.

FILE HANDLING

The **File** menu is used for all operations on files. The file commands common to every **File** menu are outlined below. The **File** menu in Figure 27 appears when no files are currently open.

When a Works tool is open, additional commands in this menu appear; they relate, for example, to printing and page and margin settings. Standard file-handling commands, however, are available in all **File** menus and are discussed in this section.

OPENING AND CLOSING FILES

CREATE NEW FILE

Figure 27. The *Create New File* command in the **File** menu allows you to create a new file. It is used to create a word processor document, spreadsheet, or database from scratch.

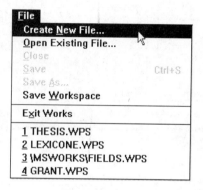

Figure 28. When this command is selected, the *Create New File* dialog box will appear. This dialog box contains four buttons—three of which represent the type of files that can be created—word processor, spreadsheet, and database.

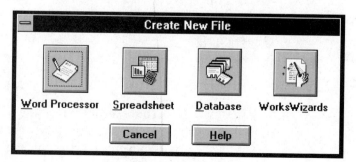

The fourth button enables you to invoke the *WorksWizards*. WorksWizards are automated templates designed to create files of various kinds. For example, you may need an address book that contains the names and addresses of all your clients. Instead of creating this yourself, you can use WorksWizards to guide you through the process.

OPEN EXISTING FILE

An existing file can be opened if it has been previously stored on disk. A file is stored on disk when it is saved.

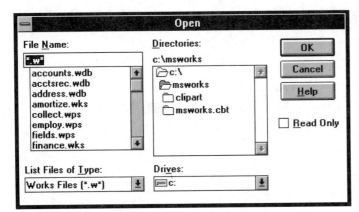

Figure 29. When the *Open Existing File* command is selected from the **File** menu, the *Open* dialog box appears on screen. From this dialog box you can choose the name of the file in the *File Name* list box, using the scroll bars if necessary. When you find the name of the file you want to open, click on it and then on *OK* to load the file into memory.

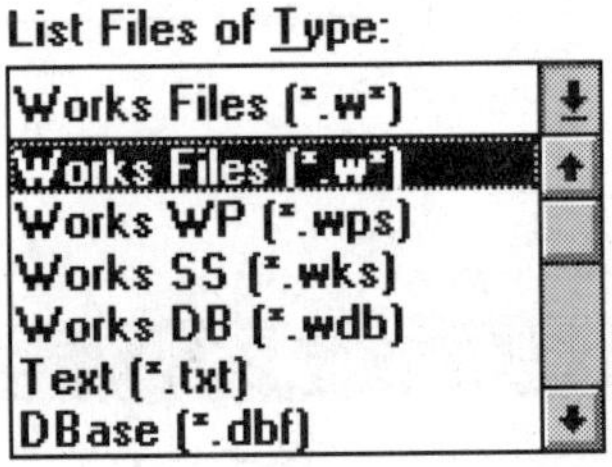

Figure 30. The *File Name* text box in Figure 29 initially displays (*.w*), so that all files with an extension beginning with "w" are displayed. All files created in Works have an extension starting with "w" and will therefore be displayed.

To specify more precisely which files you want to appear in the *File Name* list box, you can use the *List Files of Type* submenu. To view only the database files, for instance, select *Works DB (*.wdb)* from the menu and only the database files would appear, making the selection of a file much easier.

Figure 31. The *Directories* list box in the *Open* dialog box allows you to locate a file that is in another directory. A series of folders is shown representing subdirectories. To open a subdirectory, double-click on the name of the one you want to open. A list of all files within that subdirectory will appear in the *File Name* list box of Figure 29.

Directories:

c:\msworks

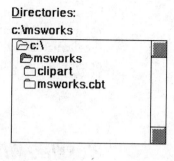

Figure 32. The disk from which Works reads the file names can be changed through the *Drives* submenu. By using this option, you can open a file that may have been saved on another hard disk or a floppy disk.

When the *Read Only* option is selected, a file can be opened but no permanent changes can be made. You can use this option to avoid the risk of changing important documents accidentally.

Dri**ve**s:

   c:

☐ **R**ead Only

FILE NAMES IN THE FILE MENU

Figure 33. A short cut for opening recently used files is through the list of files in the **File** menu. Works keeps track of the last four files that were opened and lists them at the foot of the **File** menu. Works even recalls the files open in the previous session, meaning that even though Works may have been shut down, the last files used will still be listed.

File	
Create **N**ew File...	
Open Existing File...	
Close	
Save	
Save **A**s...	
Save **W**orkspace	
Print Pre**v**iew	
Print...	Ctrl+P
Page Setup & Margins...	
Set Print Area	
P**r**inter Setup...	
E**x**it Works	
1 AMORTIZE.WKS	
2 COLLECT.WPS	
3 ACCTSREC.WDB	
4 AUDIENCE.WPS	

To open a file listed in the **File** menu, you can click on the file name or press the underlined prefix number corresponding to the file name you want. These methods have the same effect as opening a file through the *Open Existing File* command.

WORKING WITH MULTIPLE FILES

Works allows you to have a number of files open simultaneously. This is a very handy feature when you are working with a number of files that are related to each other. For instance, you may be creating a report in the Word Processor and want to copy a chart from a spreadsheet file. Works simplifies this process by allowing up to eight files to be open at once.

You can open additional files at any time in Works by using the *Create New File* or *Open Existing File* commands. Works will load files—either new or existing—into a separate window. The name of the file is displayed in the Title Bar of each window. Only one file is active at a time, but you can easily switch between files using the **Window** menu.

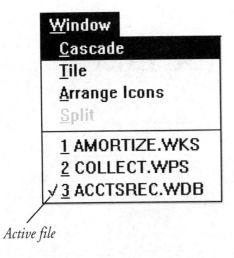

Active file

Figure 34. All Works files that are currently open are listed in the **Window** menu. To access one of these open files, just click on its file name or press the underlined numeral in front of the file name. The active file is marked with a check mark.

Figure 35. The **Window** menu is also used to change the layout of the screen using the *Tile* and *Cascade* commands. In this figure, three different files are open and are tiled on the screen. This is achieved with the *Tile* command.

The *Cascade* command displays each window stacked one behind the other, with the Title Bar and a small section of the left-hand side of each window visible.

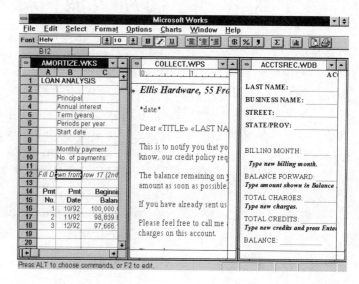

CLOSING A FILE

The *Close* command in the **File** menu terminates work on the active file and clears the screen if this is the only file open. If more than one file is open, the next active window will be displayed.

Figure 36. If changes made to a document have not been saved when the file is closed, a warning box appears. You will be given the opportunity to save your work before the file is closed and the changes are lost. If the document has not been saved previously and you click on *Yes*, the *Save As* dialog box will appear (see the next section for details).

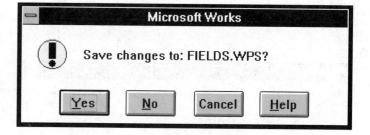

SAVING YOUR WORK

If you wish to use a document created in any software package again, it is essential to write (or save) the information to disk. Works is no different in this regard and follows a similar saving procedure to other Windows products.

Once a file has been saved, it is essential to resave your work regularly to avoid losing it by accident or through computer malfunction. Resaving the file replaces the file created on disk with the most recent version of the document.

There are two commands in the **File** menu, *Save* and *Save As*, which are used at different times when saving files. They are outlined below.

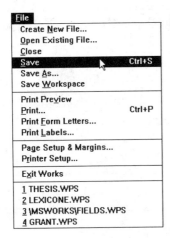

SAVE

Figure 37. The *Save* command, when activated, updates a previously saved file with the current version of the document. The *Save* command, therefore, is used to save the current document under its existing file name. The keyboard shortcut for activating this command is Ctrl+S.

If the *Save* command is chosen before a file is given a name officially, the *Save As* dialog box will appear automatically.

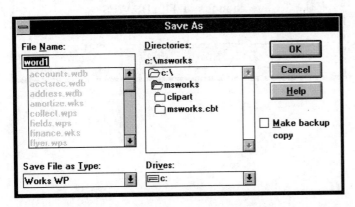

SAVE AS

Figure 38. To save a file that has not been saved before, you can choose either the *Save* or the *Save As* command. Either command will display the *Save As* dialog box if the file has not yet been saved.

When the *Save As* dialog box first appears, the text in the *File Name* text box is highlighted. This text is the file name given by Works automatically. The file name depends on the tool in which it was created and the number of files of that type that you have opened in that session. Word1, for example, tells you that you are working with the first Word Processor document opened since Works was started up.

To save a file using your choice of name, type its new name into the *File Name* text box. The file name can have up to eight characters and cannot include any spaces. Works will automatically append the correct extension for the tool you are using.

Before you click on *OK*, ensure that the file is going to be saved on the correct disk in the correct subdirectory, changing the subdirectory where necessary. When *OK* is clicked, the document is saved as a file on disk in the location specified.

Figure 39. The *Save As* option is also used to change the name of an existing file. The original file is not discarded when you use this method. You will have two copies of the same file, each with a different name. This ensures that you keep your original file, as well as a file with your latest modifications. In addition, the *Save As* command can be used to change file specifications—such as the file type.

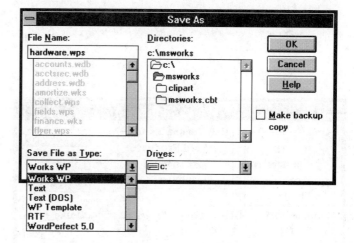

SAVE WORKSPACE

The *Save Workspace* command saves the contents of the current desktop, which may include a number of related files that are open simultaneously. *Save Workspace* can be used if you are working on a project and want Works to automatically open all the relevant files when you next start Works.

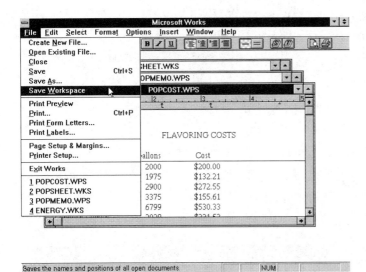

Figure 40. To use this command, you need to open all the files to be saved in the Workspace. Works does not allow you to include files that have not yet been saved as part of the Workspace, so make sure that all files have been saved through the *Save As* dialog box (Figure 38).

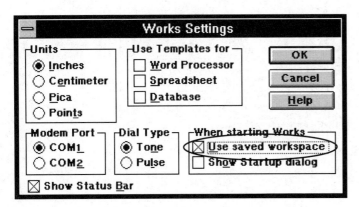

Figure 41. When you choose the *Save Workspace* command, all opened files will be saved as a set. Works will open all these files automatically the next time it is started. The *Use saved workspace* option is selected in the *Works Settings* dialog box automatically when a workspace is saved. (This dialog box is activated by choosing *Works Settings* from the **Options** menu.)

EXIT WORKS

Figure 42. The *Exit Works* command in the **File** menu will terminate your current Works session and return you to the Program Manager in Windows.

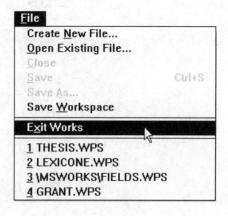

Figure 43. If any documents have not been saved when you choose *Exit Works*, Works will warn you that the file has been altered and that the changes have not been saved. To save the file at this point, click on *Yes*. To close the file and lose the changes, click on *No*. The *Cancel* button will return you to the document, aborting the *Exit Works* procedure.

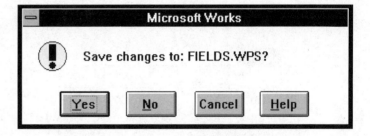

The *Help* button will activate the Help facility, giving you extra information on this topic.

BASIC EDITING

SELECTING TEXT

Before text can be edited, it must be highlighted, or selected. You can do this in various ways, either with the mouse or from the keyboard. Highlighting methods vary between tools. For specific details, refer to the section appropriate for the tool you wish to use.

CUT, COPY, AND PASTE

The *Cut, Copy,* and *Paste* commands allow you to alter the layout of a document. These commands are common to all tools in Works and function in basically the same way in each. The major difference is the type of data cut or copied. In the Spreadsheet, for example, cell contents are manipulated. In the Database, the arrangement of fields is altered, whereas the Word Processor is concerned with text and graphics.

Edit	
Undo	Alt+BkSp
Cut	Ctrl+X
Copy	Ctrl+C
Paste	Ctrl+V
Paste Special...	
Delete	Del
Object	
Links...	
Headers & Footers...	

Figure 44. Once the data is selected, basic editing is done using three commands in the **Edit** menu—*Cut, Copy,* and *Paste. Cut* will remove the selected data from the screen and place it in the Windows Clipboard. *Copy* places the highlighted selection in the Clipboard, but leaves the original selection in place.

After you have moved the insertion point to the new location, *Paste* retrieves a copy of the contents of the Clipboard and places it in your document.

HEADERS AND FOOTERS

A header is text that prints at the top of one or more pages. A footer prints text at the bottom of a page. Works has a standard type of header and footer, which is available in all tools.

Standard headers and footers allow only one line of text, which is typed into the appropriate text box. An additional *paragraph* type of header and footer is available only in the Word Processor—see Chapter 3 for details.

Figure 45. To insert headers and footers in a document, select the *Headers & Footers* command from the **Edit** menu.

Edit	
<u>U</u>ndo	Alt+BkSp
Cu<u>t</u>	Ctrl+X
<u>C</u>opy	Ctrl+C
<u>P</u>aste	Ctrl+V
Paste <u>S</u>pecial...	
<u>D</u>elete	Del
Object	
Links...	
<u>H</u>eaders & Footers...	

Figure 46. Header and footer text is typed directly into the *Headers & Footers* dialog box. The header prints, at the top of the page, what is entered in the *Header* text box, and the footer inserts, at the bottom of the page, what is keyed into the *Footer* text box.

Headers & Footers	
H<u>e</u>ader: `This is the Header text`	OK
<u>F</u>ooter `This is the Footer text`	Cancel
☐ <u>N</u>o header on 1st page ☐ <u>U</u>se header and	Help
☐ N<u>o</u> footer on 1st page footer paragraph	

```
┌─────────────────────────────────────────────────────┐
│ ▬            Headers & Footers                       │
├─────────────────────────────────────────────────────┤
│  H̲eader:  &lDocument Name&r&d          ┌──────────┐ │
│                                        │    OK    │ │
│  F̲ooter:  &p|                          └──────────┘ │
│                                        ┌──────────┐ │
│  ☐ N̲o header on 1st page   ☐ U̲se header and │ Cancel │ │
│  ☐ N̲o footer on 1st page      footer paragraphs └──────────┘ │
│                                        ┌──────────┐ │
│                                        │   Help   │ │
│                                        └──────────┘ │
└─────────────────────────────────────────────────────┘
```

Figure 47. The alignment of headers and footers is centered by default. This position can be changed by the use of codes, as this figure illustrates. The header in this figure will left-align the document file name and right-align the date in short date format. The footer will automatically print page numbers in the center of the footer space.

Code	Result	Code	Result
&l	Left align characters after code	&f	Insert filename
&r	Right align characters after code	&d	Insert date
&c	Center characters after code	&n	Insert date in long format
&p	Insert page number	&t	Insert time

Figure 48. Figure 47 uses codes to align text and print system information such as page numbers and dates. All codes available in headers and footers are shown in this table.

PAGE SETUP AND MARGINS

The way that your work will appear when printed and in *Print Preview* depends on the settings in the *Page Setup & Margins* dialog box. To access this dialog box, choose *Page Setup & Margins* from the **File** menu.

The settings that can be altered in this dialog box (Figure 49) are:

- Paper size

- Top and bottom margins

- Left and right margins

- Header and footer margins

- 1st page number

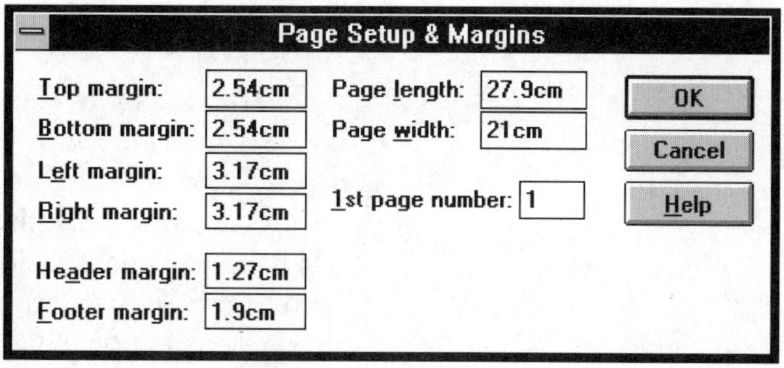

Figure 49. Units of measure in Works may be entered as inches (" or in) or as centimeters (cm). If the unit of measurement is inches, for example, and you want a setting to be in centimeters, Works will convert to the metric setting automatically.

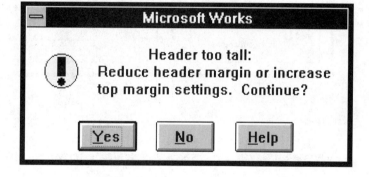

Figure 50. Header and footer margins need be altered only when the dialog box in this figure appears. These margins take up space within the top and bottom page margins. Occasionally there is a conflict between the amount of space required by the printer and the margin specification.

To work properly, header and footer margins must always be smaller than the top and bottom margins of the page. The defaults of 0.5" and 0.75" should be suitable, in most printers, for headers and footers of one line.

The *1st page number* text box under the page measurements allows you to specify the starting number for the first page.

PRINTING

Before you can print, you need to have your printer set up correctly in Windows. If you receive an error message when accessing *Print Preview* or *Print*, it is usually because printer settings do not agree with page setup and margin settings. You will be given options to alter either of these settings. If you need to alter the page setup and margin settings, refer back to the previous section.

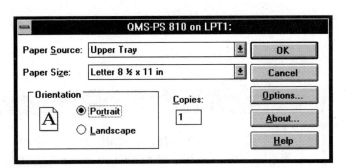

Figure 51. Printer settings can be altered by choosing *Printer Setup* from the **File** menu. The options in the *Printer Setup* dialog box should be adjusted to suit your hardware specifications.

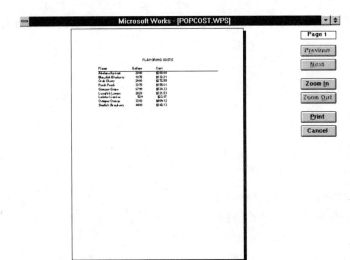

Figure 52. Before printing your document to paper, it is a good idea to print it to the screen first.

The *Print Preview* command in the **File** menu enables you to do this. By viewing the document in *Print Preview*, you can see the document as it will actually appear when printed. If there are any major faults in layout, for instance, these can be discovered and corrected before the printer is activated. This can save a lot of time and paper!

Figure 53. To print your document, select *Print* from the File menu or use the shortcut key—Ctrl+P. The *Print* dialog box appears, in which you can alter the default print settings.

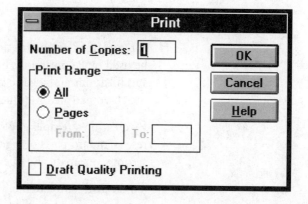

Figure 54. Works will print, by default, one copy of the complete document. To change this default, type in the number of copies required in the *Number of Copies* text box. Works will print the entire document by default. If you don't want to print the whole document, click on *Pages* and fill in the page range in the *From* and *To* boxes.

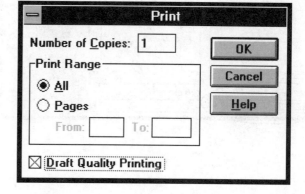

Draft Quality Printing is available only in some printers. This option prints a document quickly, omitting many of the formatting changes as it is being printed.

When you have made the changes required to the *Print* dialog box, click on *OK* to print the document.

TEMPLATES

A template is a standard document, which, once created, can be used on a continuous basis. A template file can contain page specifications and a basic layout for a particular document, which you create on numerous occasions.

By creating a template, you save yourself time by not having to reset standard parts of a document. A template will insert these settings automatically in every new document you create.

To create a template file, you start a new file and make all the changes that you want included in the template. These can contain adjustments to margins, paper size, font and font size, or even the printer.

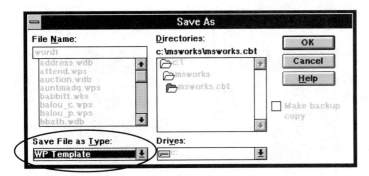

Figure 55. Once created, the file then needs to be saved as a template by selecting *Save As* from the **File** menu. When saving, click on *Save File as Type* and choose the template option. Works will save the file as *"template"* and append an appropriate extension. The extensions are *"ps"* for the Word Processor, *"wk"* for the Spreadsheet, and *"db"* for the Database.

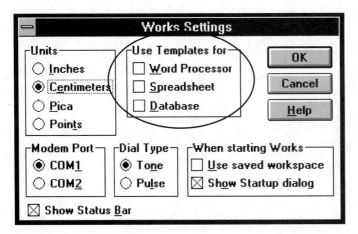

Figure 56. Saving the file as a template automatically updates *Works Settings* in the **Options** menu, selecting the *Use Templates for* check box for the appropriate file type. Works will use the settings saved in the template if a new file is opened when one of the template options is selected.

WORKS SETTINGS

Figure 57. Choosing the *Works Settings* command in the **Options** menu displays the *Works Settings* dialog box. This dialog box enables you to set certain defaults that affect the Works program.

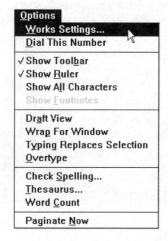

Figure 58. The *Units* group allows you to specify the unit of measure used in margins and tabs, etc. Clicking on a radio button will select that option and simultaneously deselect the previous choice.

The *Use Templates for* section is where templates can be activated if they have been created. Refer to the previous **Templates** section for more details.

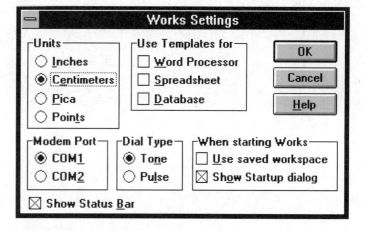

Figure 59. The *Modem Port* and *Dial Type* sections enable you to set the communications options. These apply only if you intend to use a communications device such as a modem to communicate with other computers.

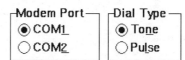

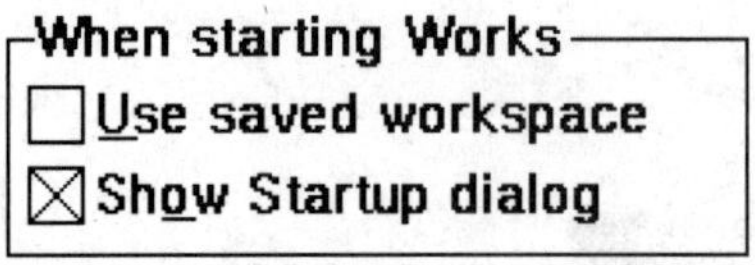

┌─When starting Works──────────┐
│ ☐ U̲se saved workspace   │
│ ☒ Sh̲ow Startup dialog   │
└──────────────────────────────┘

Figure 60. The *When starting Works* option specifies whether Works is to start by using a saved workspace or through the *Startup* dialog box (Figure 2). A cross in one of these boxes indicates that the option is active.

 ☒ **Show Status B̲ar**

Figure 61. The *Show Status Bar* option in the *Works Settings* dialog box allows you to specify whether the Status Bar is to be displayed on screen.

WORD PROCESSOR 3

INTRODUCTION

The general purpose writing tool for creating letters, memos, reports, or any other written document on a personal computer is the word processor. One of the tools in Works is a powerful word processing package that enables you to create the documents you require. In addition to creating basic documents, you can use the more advanced features—such as indenting, adding borders to paragraphs, and checking the spelling—in the Word Processor tool to give your documents added polish.

Microsoft Draw is an addition to the Works Word Processor tool that enables you to create graphics—perhaps your company logo—and import them into your document easily. The Draw package and many other useful features of the Works Word Processor are outlined in this chapter.

STARTING THE WORD PROCESSOR

The first step in activating the Word Processor is to start Works from the Windows program manager.

Figure 1. Once loaded, Works will display the *Startup* dialog box. From the *Startup* dialog box, click on the *Word Processor* button. Alternatively, click on the **File** menu and then the *Create New File* command if you have already started Works.

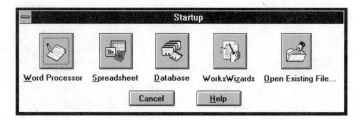

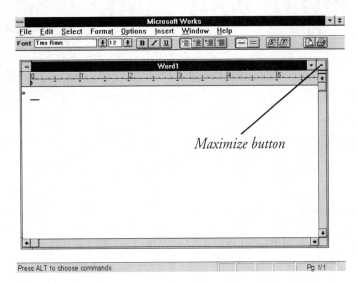

Maximize button

Figure 2. Your Word Processor screen should look similar to the one shown here. You should see the Word Processor document window inside the application window. By default, the document window is not maximized. You may want to maximize it by clicking on the Maximize button in the document window. By doing this, you can use as much of the screen area as is available.

Title Bar   *Menu Bar*   *Toolbar*   *Ruler*

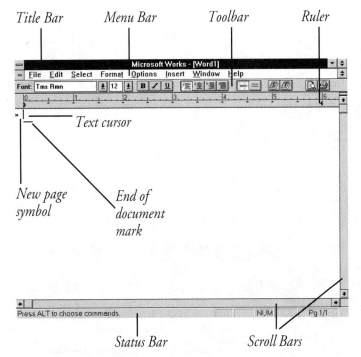

Text cursor

New page symbol   *End of document mark*

Status Bar   *Scroll Bars*

Figure 3. The components of your screen may be slightly different, depending on the commands selected in the **Options** menu. If the Toolbar is not showing, for instance, choose *Show Toolbar* from the **Options** menu to display it on the screen as in Figure 2.

If the ruler is not displayed, select **Options,** then *Show Ruler.* The ruler is particularly useful for quickly changing the tab settings in your document. The units displayed on the ruler are those that you have specified through the *Works Settings* command in the **Options** menu.

Figure 4. There are two important symbols in the blank editing screen—the text cursor and the mouse cursor. The text cursor, or insertion point, is represented by a flashing line on the screen. It is important to be aware if its position at all times, because it indicates where new characters will be inserted or where editing will take place in a document.

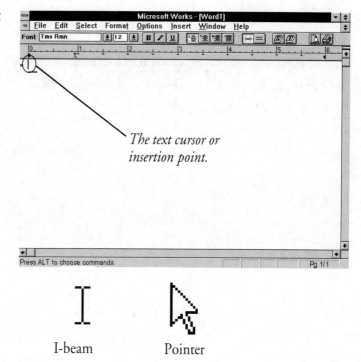

The text cursor or insertion point.

Figure 5. The mouse pointer changes shape according to its position on the screen. When the mouse cursor is in the editing screen, it is represented as an *I-beam*. It changes shape once it is moved to other parts of the screen, such as the ruler or the Menu Bar. In these areas, the mouse pointer usually turns into an arrow, or "pointer," as shown.

I-beam   Pointer

Figure 6. The heavy underline symbol on the screen marks the end of a document. It moves up and down the screen as you insert and remove text. This mark cannot be deleted and it is impossible to move the text cursor past this point.

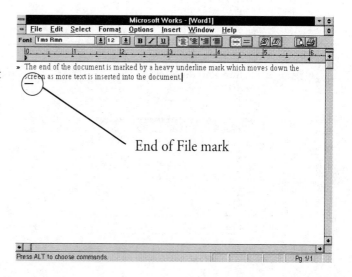

End of File mark

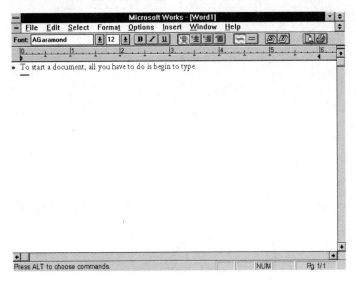

INSERTING TEXT

Figure 7. To start a document, all you need do is begin to type. In a new document, the text cursor is in the top left-hand corner of the screen. The text you type in is inserted from this point.

It is not necessary to press Enter to start a new line because Works uses a *text wrap* feature. This means that when the text reaches the end of the line—the right margin—it will automatically wrap onto the next line. The only time you need to press Enter when inserting text is when a new paragraph is required.

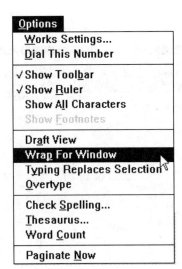

WRAP FOR WINDOW

Figure 8. *Wrap For Window* in the **Options** menu, when selected, wraps text using the edge of the screen as the guide rather than the right margin. *Wrap For Window* does not affect the margins of a document when printed, because it is only used for screen layout.

This feature is best activated when the screen is too narrow to show an entire line of text on the page—when you are using a landscape page, for example.

DRAFT VIEW

A document that contains a number of different fonts and font styles can often take time to redraw on the screen. Because of this, Works offers *a Draft View* mode, which is selected through the **Options** menu.

Figure 9. When the screen is displayed in Draft View, only one font and font size is applied, making working with a large document much quicker.

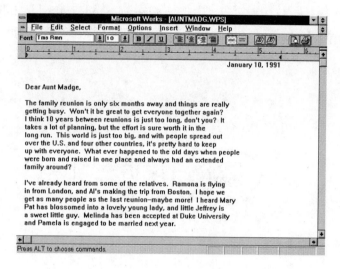

SHOW ALL CHARACTERS

Works inserts special characters to mark parts of a specific document. For instance, when text is wrapped onto a new line, a soft return mark—indicated by a left arrow—is inserted into the document.

Figure 10. By default, Works does not show these special characters. They can be viewed by selecting *Show All Characters* from the **Options** menu. There are numerous special characters, some of which are displayed in this figure.

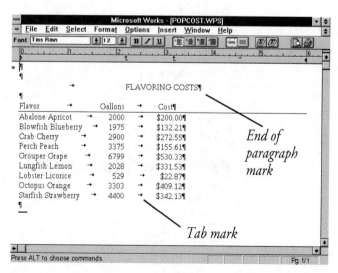

INSERT AND OVERTYPE MODE

When in *Insert* mode, characters typed into the document automatically push any text to the right of the text cursor, further along the line. This is the default setting in Works, and should be used most of the time.

Overtype mode is used mainly when editing text in a document. New text being keyed into a document will replace—or type over—any text that is currently to the right of the cursor.

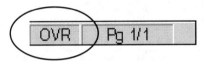

Figure 11. Overtype mode is activated by pressing the Insert key. The Insert key acts as a toggle switch between Insert and Overtype modes. When Overtype is active, the letters "OVR" appear on the right side of the Status Bar.

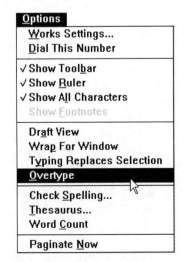

Figure 12. Overtype mode can be turned on and off using the Insert key on the keyboard. Selecting and deselecting the *Overtype* command in the **Options** menu performs the same function.

MOVING THE CURSOR

You can move the cursor around a word processor document by using the keyboard or the mouse. Both are very efficient, so the best one to use is the one that is most convenient at the time!

USING THE MOUSE

Figure 13. To move the text cursor using the mouse, simply position the I-beam in the required position in the text and click the left mouse button. The flashing text cursor is automatically placed wherever the I-beam is clicked.

Figure 14. If you need to move the cursor to a part of the document that cannot be seen on the screen, use the scroll bars to move through the document and then follow the same procedure of clicking the I-beam.

USING THE KEYBOARD

Figure 15. The text cursor is moved in the document using a combination of cursor keys on the keyboard. This table lists quick ways to move the cursor within a word processor document using the keyboard.

Key	Cursor Movement	Key	Cursor Movement
Left arrow	Left one character	Right arrow	Right one character
Up arrow	Up one line	Down arrow	Down one line
Ctrl+left arrow	Left one word	Ctrl+right arrow	Right one word
Ctrl+up arrow	Up one paragraph	Ctrl+down arrow	Down one paragraph
Home	Beginning of line	End	End of line
Ctrl+Home	Beginning of document	Ctrl+End	End of Document
Page Up	Up one screen	Page Down	Down one screen
Ctrl+Page Up	Start of screen	Ctrl+Page Down	End of Screen

THE GO TO COMMAND

Figure 16. The *Go To* command allows you to move quickly to a particular place in your document. This position is marked by bookmarks.

The *Go To* command can be activated in one of two ways:

- By selecting the *Go To* command in the **Select** menu (as shown)

- By pressing F5

The *Go To* feature, however, is not usable until the Word Processor document contains bookmarks. A bookmark is a hidden marker inserted into a document to mark an important place.

A bookmark is usually a point in the document to which you often refer back. To save your having to constantly scroll through the document to find this place—the start of a new section, perhaps—you can insert a bookmark and use *Go To* to move there quickly.

Figure 17. To insert a bookmark, move the cursor to the place you want to mark in the document. In this case, the bookmark inserted will mark the part in the résumé document that refers to the "ADVERTISING" section.

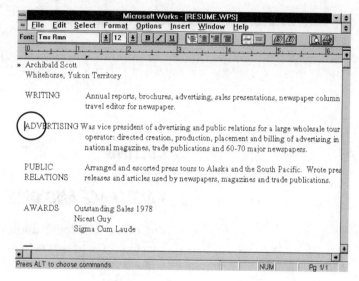

Figure 18. The menu command to insert a bookmark is *Bookmark Name* in the **Insert** menu. This command displays the *Bookmark Name* dialog box.

The name of the new bookmark is keyed into the *Name* text box. When you click on *OK*, it becomes part of the document and you can use it with the *Go To* feature.

Names of existing bookmarks in the document are listed in the *Names* list box. This example shows another two— Writing and Awards.

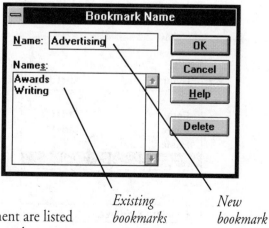

Existing bookmarks   *New bookmark*

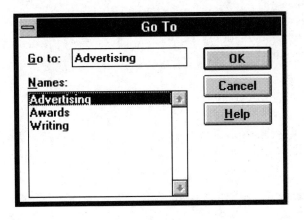

Figure 19. The bookmarks can now be used in conjunction with the *Go To* feature. When you select *Go To* in a document containing bookmarks, the bookmarks will be listed in the *Names* list box as shown here.

To move to any one of these bookmarks, select the one you want and click on *OK*. Works will move the cursor to the part of the document marked by that bookmark.

EDITING

BACKSPACE AND DELETE

You delete text from a document by using the Backspace and Delete keys. Characters to the left of the text cursor are removed when you press Backspace.

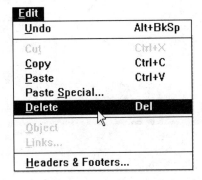

Figure 20. To remove a character to the right of the text cursor, press Delete. Alternatively, select *Delete* from the **Edit** menu. To delete a block of text, you must first highlight it (see the **Highlighting Text** section in this chapter). Once the text is highlighted, you can delete it by pressing Delete or selecting *Delete* from the **Edit** menu.

TYPING REPLACES SELECTION

Figure 21. It is sometimes easier to replace highlighted text by immediately typing in new text, rather than deleting the text first and then typing. In order to do this, select *Typing Replaces Selection* in the **Options** menu.

When this command is selected, highlighted text is removed as soon as you key in new text.

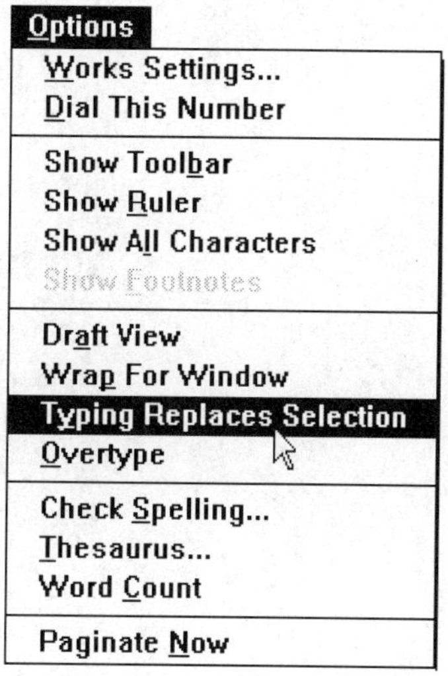

```
Options
  Works Settings...
  Dial This Number

  Show Toolbar
  Show Ruler
  Show All Characters
  Show Footnotes

  Draft View
  Wrap For Window
  Typing Replaces Selection
  Overtype

  Check Spelling...
  Thesaurus...
  Word Count

  Paginate Now
```

UNDO

Figure 22. The *Undo* command in the **Edit** menu can reverse the last activated command. However, this command must be used immediately after a command has been issued, because only the last command is affected by *Undo*.

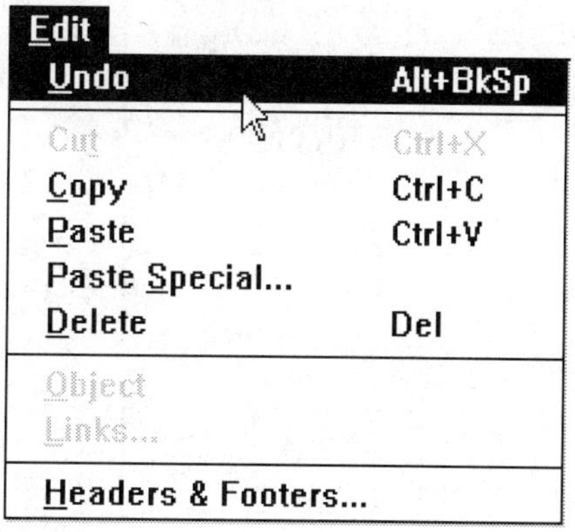

```
Edit
  Undo                  Alt+BkSp

  Cut                   Ctrl+X
  Copy                  Ctrl+C
  Paste                 Ctrl+V
  Paste Special...
  Delete                Del

  Object
  Links...

  Headers & Footers...
```

The *Undo* command—if used correctly—will restore the screen as it was before you did the *last* change. This applies to both text and formatting changes. This feature is useful for reversing the effects of any error made in your document.

HIGHLIGHTING TEXT

Highlighting text (displaying text in reverse video) is an essential part of manipulating your document. Many of the formatting capabilities require that you select text before you make any changes. You can highlight text using the mouse, the keyboard, or the **Select** menu.

THE MOUSE AND KEYBOARD

An easy technique to use when highlighting with the mouse is swiping the text. To swipe text, hold down the mouse cursor at the beginning of the text and drag over it, releasing the mouse button when the required text is highlighted.

Text can also be highlighted with the mouse through a series of clicks combined with keys.

To Highlight	Mouse	Keyboard
A word	Double-click on the word	Move to word, press F8 twice
A line	Click pointer in left margin next to line	Press F8 then Shift+End at beginning of line
A sentence	Click and drag insertion bar over sentence	Move to sentence, press F8 three times
A few lines	Drag pointer in left margin over lines	Move to lines, press F8 then Shift and Up or Down arrows
A paragraph	Double-click pointer in left margin next to paragraph	Move to paragraph, press F8 four times
The whole document	Press Ctrl and click pointer in left margin	Press F8 five times

Figure 23. The F8 key plays a dominant role in selecting text with the keyboard. Pressing F8 once—or selecting *Text* from the **Select** menu—activates the "extended cursor." Works places EXT in the Status Bar, indicating that the extended cursor is active.

Pressing F8 again highlights the word at the cursor position. If you keep pressing the F8 key—up to five times—different parts of the document are highlighted. The table shown outlines these. The extended cursor is deactivated by pressing the Escape key.

Figure 24. As displayed in Figure 23, you can select the entire document using the mouse or the keyboard. It can also be highlighted by selecting the *All* command in the **Select** menu.

FIND

Figure 25. Sometimes you need to find specific data in your document. Choosing the *Find* command from the **Select** menu will display the *Find* dialog box. To search for a word, enter the text in the *Find What* text box.

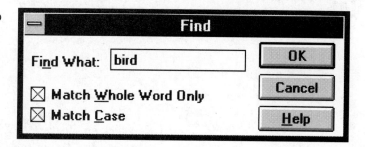

If you click in the box *Match Whole Word Only*, Works will find the text only where it appears as an entire word and not if it is part of a longer word. For example, if you typed 'the' into the *Find What* text box and selected *Match Whole Word Only*, Works would find "the," but not "mother" or "nevertheless."

Select *Match Case* if you want Works to match the capitalization entered into the *Find What* text box exactly. For example, if you typed "bird" and selected *Match Case,* Works would not find "Bird" or "BIRD."

You can also search for codes in Works, such as tabs, page breaks, or end of line marks. A page break, for example, is inserted by keying in "^d" into the *Find What* text box. These codes have to be inserted in a special way. The Help screen topic *Finding text & special characters* provides a list of all these special characters.

REPLACE

The *Replace* function is more powerful than the *Find* feature, because it allows you to find occurrences of a word, words, and special codes and replace them with other text or codes.

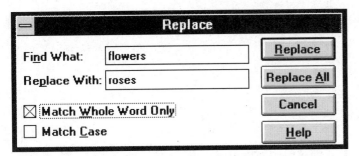

Figure 26. The *Replace* dialog box appears on screen when *Replace* is selected from the **Select** menu. Works will search for the text that is inserted into the *Find What* text box and replace it with whatever is in the *Replace With* text box. Clicking on the *Replace* button begins the *Replace* procedure, allowing you to confirm each proposed replacement.

If you click on *Replace All,* Works automatically replaces all instances of the data in the *Find What* box with what is in the *Replace With* text box. The other options in the *Replace* dialog box are the same as those in *Find.*

FORMATTING TEXT

Formatting a document alters font and font styles, indents and spacing, tabs and borders. Some of these formats affect highlighted text, some whole paragraphs, and others, the entire document.

Each of these formats is applied through the **Format** menu and is covered in the following sections. Most of the options discussed here are also available through the Toolbar; these were briefly outlined in **Chapter 2 — Common Features.**

FONT AND STYLE

Figure 27. Because font and style commands affect the appearance of text, the text to be formatted must be selected first. Selecting *Font & Style* from the **Format** menu will display the dialog box shown in Figure 28.

FONT

Figure 28. Fonts available to you are listed in the *Font* list box in the *Font & Style* dialog box. The number of fonts listed depends on the printer you are using and whether any downloadable fonts have been installed.

To change the font of highlighted text, simply choose the name of the font you require from the *Font* list box and click on *OK*.

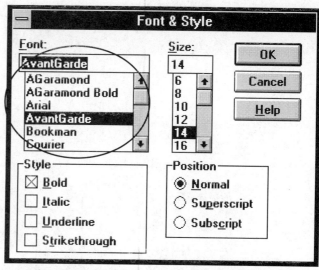

SIZE

Figure 29. You can change the point size of text by selecting the appropriate point size from the *Size* list box and clicking on *OK*. Font sizes vary according to the font selected and are also printer dependent.

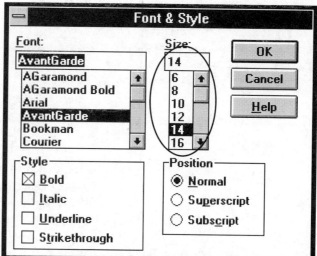

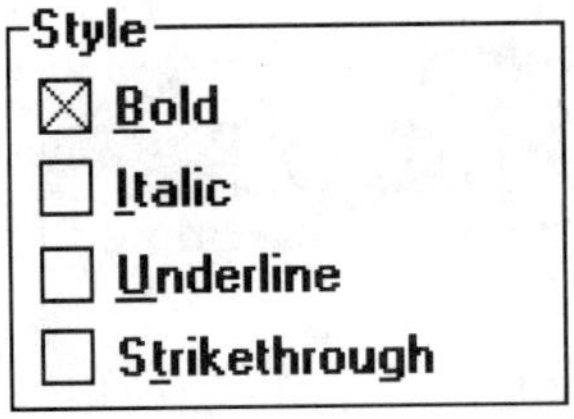

STYLE

Figure 30. The style of text can be normal, bold, italic, underlined, or strikethrough. The *Style* check boxes list all these options except normal. Normal text is applied when no check boxes are selected.

Because these check boxes are nonexclusive, more than one style can be applied to a piece of highlighted text.

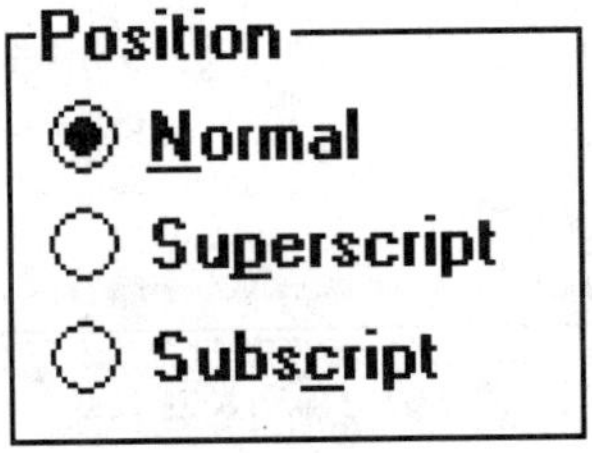

POSITION

Figure 31. The *Position* of text refers to its placement in relation to the "line" on which it is typed. The *Font & Style* dialog box gives you three position choices. The use of radio buttons indicates that these options—*Normal, Superscript,* and *Subscript*—are mutually exclusive.

Superscript is applied to highlighted text to raise it slightly above the normal placement of text. For example, the degrees symbol in $15°$ is in the superscript position. Subscript is the reverse, placing text slightly below the normal position—for example, the "2" in H_2O.

Figure 32. The shortcuts available for applying *Font & Style* options are outlined in the table to the right.

Action	Result	Action	Result
Ctrl+B	Bold	Ctrl+=	Subscript
Ctrl+U	Underline	Ctrl+Shift+=	Superscript
Ctrl+I	Italics	Ctrl+Spacebar	Remove font styles
Ctrl+F	Open Font sub-menu	Ctrl+Z	Open Size sub-menu

INDENTS AND SPACING

Figure 33. The options in the *Indents & Spacing* dialog box (**Format** menu) affect entire paragraphs of text. A paragraph is a piece of text enclosed by paragraph marks. You can select a paragraph by following the instructions outlined in the **Highlighting Text** section of this chapter, or simply by clicking the text cursor in the paragraph to be formatted.

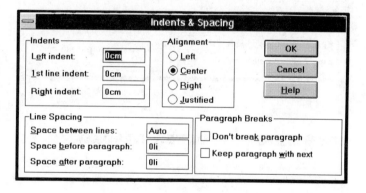

Select *Indents & Spacing* from the **Format** menu to display the *Indents & Spacing* dialog box. You can apply a number of formats using this dialog box: indenting, aligning, line spacing, and paragraph breaks.

INDENTS

Indents provide you with a means of organizing a document. A document with indented paragraphs is more readable because it is much easier to locate information.

There a number of different kinds of indents, but the basic idea behind indenting is that the right or left margin is moved in or out, directly affecting the amount of text that can fit between those margins.

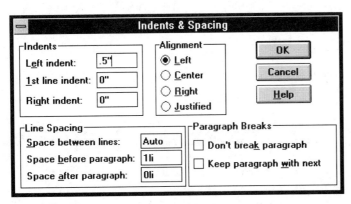

Figure 34. To move the whole paragraph in from the left margin, key in the distance at which the paragraph is to be indented into the *Left indent* text box in the *Indents & Spacing* dialog box. In this case, a left indent of .5 inches will be applied to the selected paragraph when you click on *OK*.

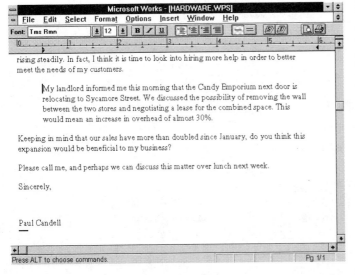

Figure 35. The result of the .5-inch left indent is shown in this figure. Notice also that the indent markers on the left side of the ruler have moved to the .5-inch position.

The left indent marker is actually made up of two sections—the first line indent (top) and the rest of paragraph indent (bottom).

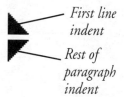

First line indent

Rest of paragraph indent

Indent marks can be moved on the ruler without having to open the *Indents & Spacing* dialog box. They can simply be dragged to the new position, affecting the indent of the selected paragraph.

Figure 36. Another indent that is useful when you are listing items is a hanging indent. This can be created in three ways in Works: using the *Indents & Spacing* dialog box, moving the indent markers on the ruler, or pressing Ctrl+H for each indentation level.

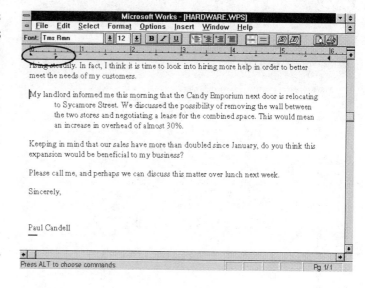

When a hanging indent is first applied—0.5 of an inch, for example—the first line remains at zero and the rest of the paragraph is indented 0.5 inches. The indent markers on the ruler reflect these values.

Figure 37. A hanging indent can be used to create a bulleted or numbered list. To produce the result of this figure, perform the following steps:

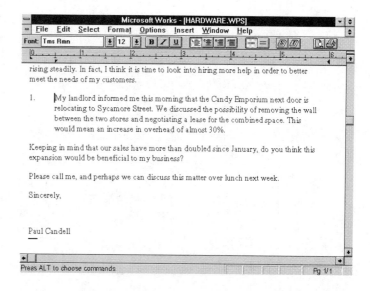

(a) move the cursor to the first line of the paragraph

(b) Key in 1. and press Tab

(c) Press Ctrl+H

Indent Type	Turn On	Turn Off
Left Indent	Ctrl+N	Ctrl+M
Hanging Indent	Ctrl+H	Ctrl+G

Figure 38. To set indents using keyboard shortcuts, follow the commands shown in this table.

ALIGN

Figure 39. There are four types of alignment available in Works. These are *Left* (the default), *Right, Center,* and *Justified.* As with changing indents, the text cursor must be located in the paragraph to be formatted. You then select the type of alignment required in the *Indents & Spacing* dialog box (Figure 34).

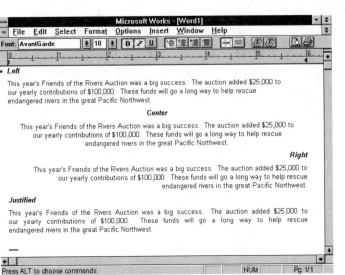

Action	Result
Ctrl+L	Left align
Ctrl+R	Right align
Ctrl+J	Justify
Ctrl+E	Center

Figure 40. Alignment can also be changed by clicking on the *Alignment* buttons on the Toolbar or using the shortcuts outlined in this table.

LINE SPACING

Figure 41. You can add extra space between lines in a paragraph by keying a number into the *Space between lines* text box in the *Indents & Spacing* dialog box. Alternatively, you can use the *Line Spacing* buttons on the Toolbar to apply either double or single spacing.

Indents & Spacing
Indents
Left indent: 0"
1st line indent: 0"
Right indent: 0"
Alignment
Left
Center
Right
Justified
OK
Cancel
Help
Line Spacing
Space between lines: Auto
Space before paragraph: 0li
Space after paragraph: 0li
Paragraph Breaks
Don't break paragraph
Keep paragraph with next

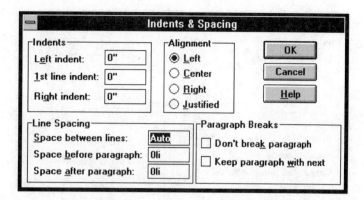

In standard word processors, you need to press Enter a few times at the end of a paragraph to separate it from the paragraph below. This method adds extra "End-of-Paragraph" codes to a document, which can create problems. Extra codes can be avoided by adding the extra space required using the *Space before paragraph* and *Space after paragraph* options in the *Indents & Spacing* dialog box.

Two line spaces are added after the paragraph.

Figure 42. To insert an extra two lines at the end of a paragraph, for instance, highlight the paragraph—Dear Ms. Rogers, in this case—and type "2" into the *Space after paragraph* text box shown in Figure 41.

When you click on *OK*, the following paragraph is moved down the page two line spaces from the paragraph above it.

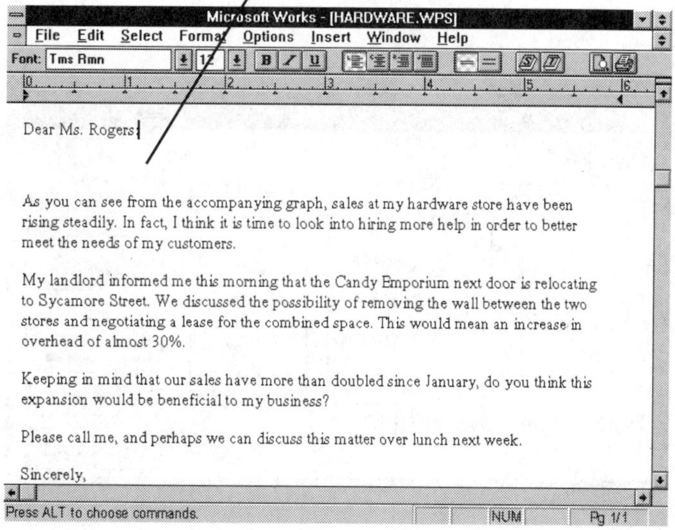

Microsoft Works - [HARDWARE.WPS]
File Edit Select Format Options Insert Window Help
Font: Tms Rmn
Dear Ms. Rogers:
As you can see from the accompanying graph, sales at my hardware store have been rising steadily. In fact, I think it is time to look into hiring more help in order to better meet the needs of my customers.
My landlord informed me this morning that the Candy Emporium next door is relocating to Sycamore Street. We discussed the possibility of removing the wall between the two stores and negotiating a lease for the combined space. This would mean an increase in overhead of almost 30%.
Keeping in mind that our sales have more than doubled since January, do you think this expansion would be beneficial to my business?
Please call me, and perhaps we can discuss this matter over lunch next week.
Sincerely,
Press ALT to choose commands.
NUM
Pg 1/1

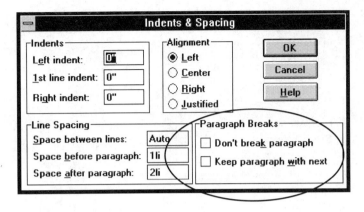

Figure 43. The *Paragraph Breaks* section allows you overcome the problem of paragraphs being split by an automatic page break. When *Don't break paragraph* is active, the selected paragraph will not be broken by a page break. The entire paragraph will be moved onto the next page.

Keep paragraph with next enables you to keep two related paragraphs together. This option is often applied to enhance the readability of a document.

TABS

Tabs are added to a document to space text evenly—for instance, in tables and lists. There are a number of tab types, all of which are covered in this section. Tabs can be inserted through the *Tabs* dialog box, which is opened either by selecting *Tabs* from the **Format** menu or by double-clicking on the ruler. It is best to click on the top half of the ruler, because clicking on the bottom half will insert an unwanted tab.

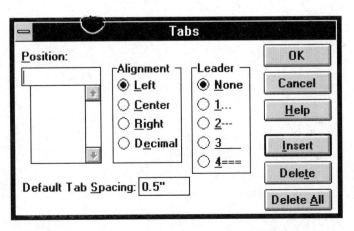

Figure 44. In the *Tabs* dialog box, you can alter all tab specifications, such as the position of a tab on the ruler, the tab's type, and whether leader characters are required.

Figure 45. There are four tab types that can be used in Works: *Left, Right, Decimal* and *Center*. You can add a style of leader, such as a row of dots, leading up to a tab position. Each type of tab is illustrated in this figure.

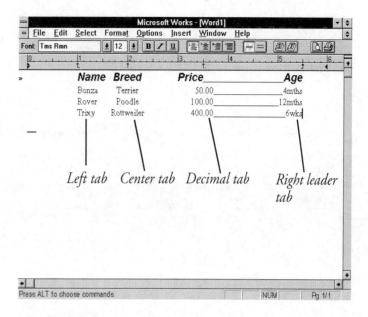

Figure 46. The tabs in Figure 45 were inserted by typing the position in the *Position* text box, selecting the type of alignment from the *Alignment* radio buttons, and choosing a leader if required. In this case, a leader was added to the right tab at 5.5 inches. After each tab specification is set, the *Insert* button must be clicked to add the tab to the document.

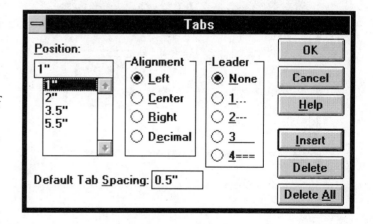

To delete all the old tabs, click on the *Delete All* button in the bottom right of the dialog box. To get evenly spaced tabs, enter a measurement in the *Default Tab Spacing* box. To return to the document, click on *OK*.

Works uses tabs settings inserted in the *Tabs* dialog box to separate text in the document. The text cursor will "jump" to the next tab stop when the Tab key is pressed.

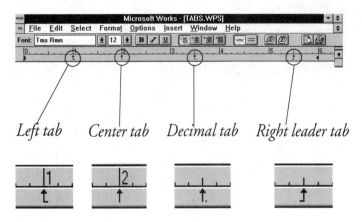

Figure 47. When tabs are added, the tab marks on the ruler are changed. Each of these arrows represents a tab mark. Left tabs can even be inserted directly onto the ruler by clicking the mouse pointer in the position of the new tab. To delete a tab from the ruler, drag the tab down into the editing screen and the tab will be removed.

Left tab   Center tab   Decimal tab   Right leader tab

BORDERS

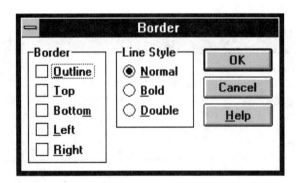

Figure 48. Works allows you to put a choice of border styles around a paragraph. After selecting the paragraph, choose *Border* from the **Format** menu to display the *Border* dialog box.

A border can enclose the paragraph completely using the *Outline* border option. It will appear on just one side of the paragraph—either *Top, Bottom, Left,* or *Right*—when one of the other options is selected. You can also use a combination of these options to create different effects.

The type of line used in the border is selected from the *Line Style* options. There are three choices—*Normal, Bold,* and *Double*.

Figure 49. This figure shows two examples of a border around a centered heading. In the first example, the border extends to the left and right margins, which creates a much wider border than necessary. In the second example, the border has been made narrower by adjusting the left and right margins only in the paragraph that contains the border.

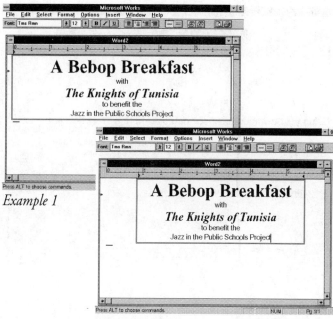

Example 1

Example 2

You can remove a border from a paragraph by deselecting all check boxes in the *Border* group in the *Border* dialog box.

PARAGRAPH HEADERS AND FOOTERS

Two types of headers and footers can be inserted into a Works Word Processor document— standard and paragraph. Standard headers and footers have been covered in **Chapter 2 — Common Features**.

Figure 50. Paragraph headers and footers are available only in the Word Processor. They are used to add headers and footers that require more than one line of text. To insert a paragraph-style header or footer, choose *Headers & Footers* from the **Edit** menu and click in the check box *Use header and footer paragraphs*.

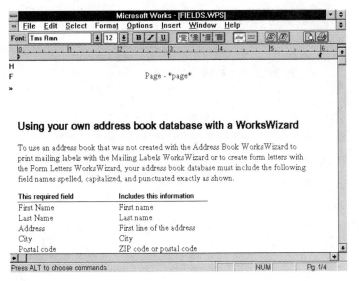

Figure 51. Paragraph headers and footers insert markers (**H** and **F**) appear at the top of the document when you click on *OK*, as shown in Figure 50.

You can insert text—or a graphic—into the header on the "H" line, which is blank by default. As the header is inserted, it will be wrapped onto the next line as necessary.

The default footer has the word "Page" and the special code, *page*, which prints sequential page numbers at the bottom of each page. You can delete this default using the Backspace key if you do not need page numbers.

If you try to Print or Print Preview a document whose header or footer margins are incompatible with the top or bottom page margins, Works will display a warning dialog box. If this happens, reduce the number of lines in your header or footer, or adjust the top or bottom margins using the *Page Setup & Margins* command in the **File** menu. (See the *Page Setup and Margins* section in **Chapter 2 — Common Features** for details about this problem.)

PAGE BREAKS

Works will decide automatically where a page break is to go according to the page size and margins you have set. However, Works does not always break pages in the most logical position for the document. You can insert manual (or hard) page breaks to specify exactly where you want a new page to begin.

Figure 52. To insert a page break, position the text cursor and select *Page Break* from the **Insert** menu. The short cut for this is to press Ctrl+Enter.

Figure 53. A dotted line will appear, representing the position of the page break. A "New page" symbol is inserted directly under the page break indicating the first line in the new page. The page reference on the Status Bar will adjust accordingly.

To remove a page break, position the cursor under the dotted line on the screen and press Backspace.

New page symbol   *Page Break*   *Page reference on Status bar*

Figure 54. Works may defer renumbering pages when a number of page breaks are inserted and deleted.

To update pagination in the document, select *Paginate Now* from the **Options** menu.

FOOTNOTES

Footnotes add extra information to a document without inserting it into the main body of the text. Footnotes, which document quotations, are common in essays and articles, and are usually referenced by a sequential numbering system.

Footnotes can also be used to highlight information in a business document—for example, a price list. A product currently out of stock could be marked with a footnote character. The footnote could inform you of this at the bottom of the page without disrupting the layout of the price list. This type of footnote would probably use a special character, such as an asterisk.

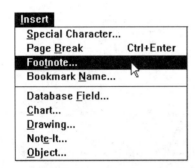

Figure 55. To insert a footnote, choose *Footnote* from the **Insert** menu.

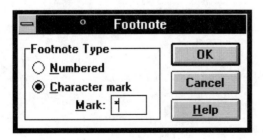

Figure 56. Works allows you to use either sequential numbers to mark the footnotes in the document or a character of your choice. The character could simply be a keyboard one, or you could use a character from the extended character set.

To insert an extended character, hold down the Alt key and type in the extended character number on the numeric keypad on your keyboard. For instance, to insert a bullet (•), hold down the Alt key and key in 0183 on the numeric keypad. These characters, however, are printer dependent. A complete list of the extended characters can be found in **Appendix B** of the **Microsoft Works User's Guide**.

Figure 57. When you have set the character to mark the footnote, click on *OK*. The document window will be split in two, providing you with a footnote pane, which is identical to a document window. Key the footnote text into the footnote pane where the character mark has been automatically inserted. Default tabs are set, which can be used to organize the text.

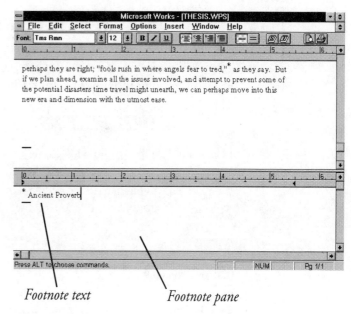

Footnote text   *Footnote pane*

To move back to your document, click in the document window or press F6. The footnote pane is closed by deselecting *Show Footnotes* in the **Options** menu. If you need to view the footnotes again—perhaps to edit an existing footnote—select *Show Footnotes*.

Figure 58. The footnote text appears at the bottom of the page in *Print Preview* and when the document is printed. The reference mark appears in front of the text as well as in the document itself.

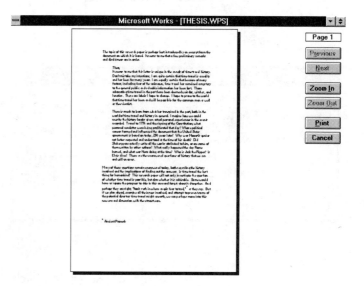

DOCUMENT ACCESSORIES

The **Options** menu contains commands to help you refine text in your document. These are the Spelling Checker, Thesaurus, and the Word Count features.

SPELL CHECKING

The spelling checker uses a 120,000-word dictionary to scan a document for words that are misspelled, capitalized or are hyphenated incorrectly. The spelling checker also looks for double occurrences of a word, such as "the the."

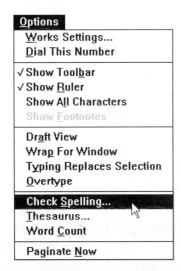

Figure 59. To activate the spell checking facility, choose the *Check Spelling* command in the **Options** menu or click on the Spelling button in the Toolbar.

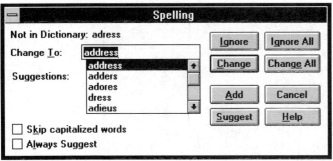

Figure 60. When Works finds a word it does not recognize, it indicates in the *Spelling* dialog box that this word is not in the dictionary. You can search the dictionary for the correct spelling of the word by clicking on the *Suggest* button. A list of suggestions will appear in the *Suggestions* list box when the search is complete.

The suggestion most likely to be correct appears in the *Change To* text box.

To choose another of the listed suggestions, click on the appropriate word in the *Suggestions* list box. Click on *Change,* and Works will alter the document and continue to check the spelling.

Skip capitalized words instructs Works to ignore words with all capitalized letters. *Always Suggest* will display suggestions automatically, so that you don't need to click on *Suggest.*

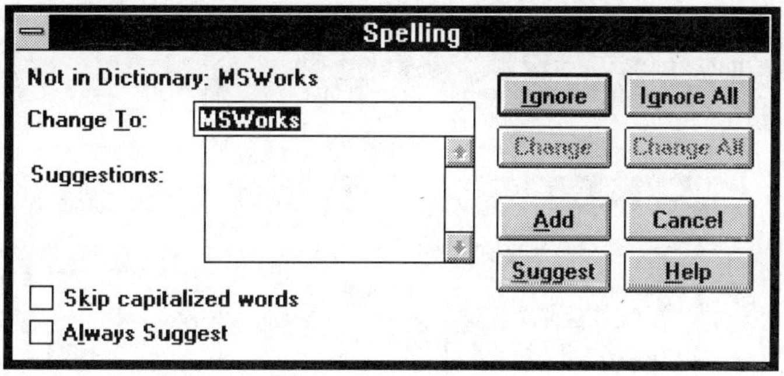

Figure 61. Works is quite powerful in that it ignores many names, such as Peter or Susan. Occasionally, however, it finds words which are spelled correctly but not in the dictionary—for example, MSWorks. You can add these words to the dictionary if you are likely to use them in many documents by clicking on *Add.* If the word will not be used often, choose *Ignore,* so that Works will ignore this occurrence of the word and continue spell checking. Choose *Ignore All* and Works won't question the word if it appears in the document again.

THESAURUS

The Thesaurus provides synonyms—words with identical or similar meanings. Using this feature can add flair to your document because you can avoid using the same word too often. There are 170,000 words available in the Thesaurus, which gives you flexibility in searching for exact meanings.

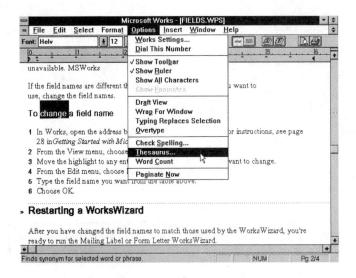

Figure 62. The Thesaurus is activated by clicking on the *Thesaurus* button or selecting *Thesaurus* from the **Options** menu. Before activating the Thesaurus, you need to select the word for which you want a synonym.

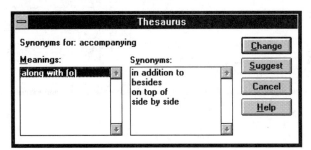

Figure 63. A list of meanings is provided in the *Meanings* list box. You select the meaning that best suits the context of the document from the *Meanings* list box. More meanings are provided if you click the *Suggest* button when a word in the *Meanings* or *Synonyms* list box is selected. Select the actual synonym to be inserted in the document from the *Synonyms* list box. When you click on *Change*, this word will replace the highlighted word on the screen.

WORD COUNT

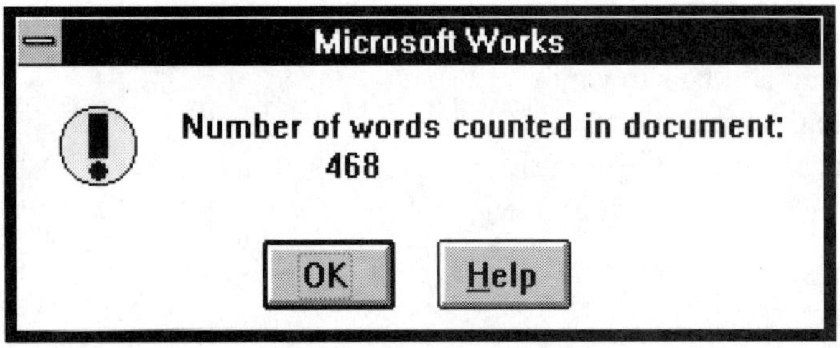

Figure 64. The *Word Count* command in the **Options** menu will count the number of words in a selection of text, or in the entire document if no text is selected. This feature helps you gauge the length of an article or assignment.

MICROSOFT DRAW

The Draw program is accessed through the Word Processor tool. It allows you to create graphic images and import them into a Works document. These could be clip art images supplied with Works, or designs that you have created yourself.

Figure 65. The *Drawing* command in the **Insert** menu activates Microsoft Draw. Before starting the Draw program, however, the cursor should be positioned where you want to insert the drawing in your document.

THE DRAW SCREEN

The Draw screen provides a series of tools and options for creating graphics. These include the Toolbar, the color palettes, and the drawing area, as well as the basic Works features such as the Menu Bar, scroll bars, and Status Bar.

THE DRAWING AREA

Figure 66. The drawing area is in the center of the screen and it is here that you import, create and edit graphics.

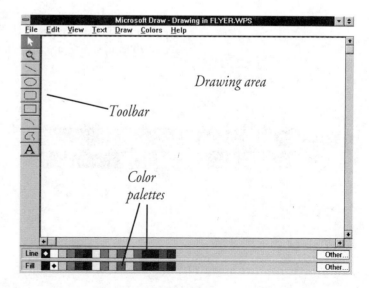

TOOLBAR

Figure 67. The Toolbar, on the left-hand side of the screen, contains nine tools, which perform different tasks in the Draw package. The arrow, for example, selects objects on the screen, and the magnifying glass is used to zoom in and out of a drawing.

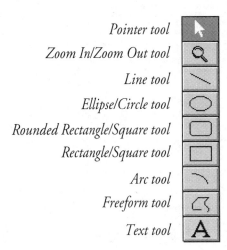

Pointer tool
Zoom In/Zoom Out tool
Line tool
Ellipse/Circle tool
Rounded Rectangle/Square tool
Rectangle/Square tool
Arc tool
Freeform tool
Text tool

The other tools on the Toolbar create objects of various shapes such as lines, circles, boxes, and arcs. The "A" tool enables you to insert text in your drawing. To select a tool, click on the one you want to use and move the mouse pointer onto the drawing area.

The mouse pointer will change shape according to the tool selected. You then click and type to insert text, or click and drag the mouse pointer to create the desired shape.

With these tools you can create complex graphics by combining basic shapes in different sizes, colors, line styles, and shadings. You are only limited by your imagination!

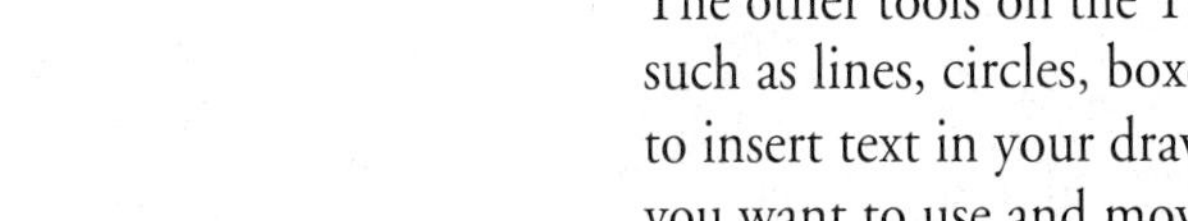

THE COLOR PALETTE

Figure 68. The color of a line and the fill of an object are easily changed using the color palette. Select the object to be altered first, then choose the color you want from the color palette.

INSERTING CLIPART

A number of predesigned graphics—called *clip art*—are a part of the Works program. When Works is installed, the clip art is copied to a subdirectory under the ***msworks*** directory called ***clipart***. Each clip art file has an extension of "*.wmf*" and can be used to enhance one of your own creations or as a drawing in its own right.

Figure 69. To insert a piece of clip art, choose *Import Picture* from the **File** menu in the Drawing program, then select one of the files with an extension of *.wmf* from the clip art subdirectory. When you click on *OK*, the clip art picture is placed in the drawing area, where you can add to it if you wish.

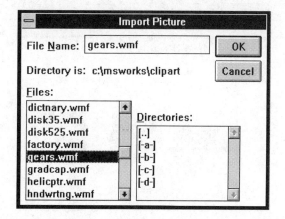

IMPORTING A DRAWING

Figure 70. When you are happy with the graphic and are ready to insert it into your Word Processor document, select *Exit and Return* from the **File** menu.

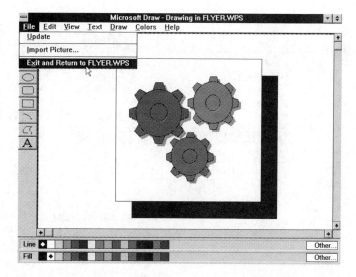

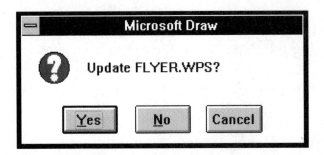

Figure 71. A dialog box will ask if you want to import the graphic and update your Word Processor document.

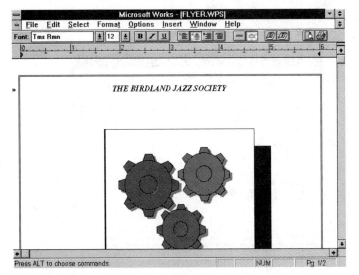

Figure 72. Click on *Yes* in the Figure 71 dialog box. The graphic now becomes part of the Word Processor document at the cursor position.

The graphic can be cut, copied, and pasted in the document just like a piece of text. The alignment of the graphic can be changed by highlighting it and selecting the type of alignment required—just like normal text.

EDITING A DRAWING

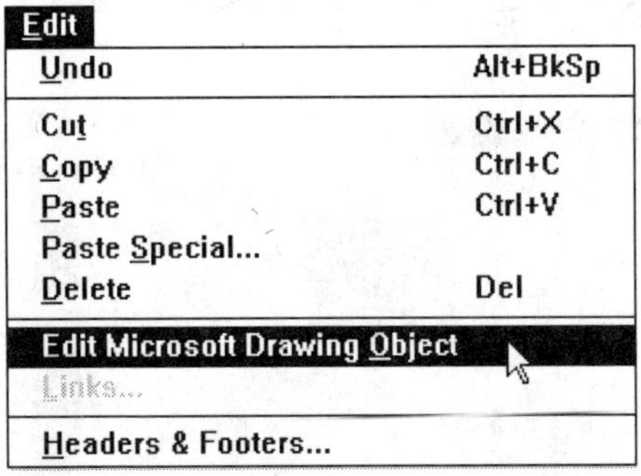

Figure 73. Should you need to edit the drawing in any way, just double-click on the graphic in the Word Processor document to restart the Drawing package. Alternatively, highlight the graphic and select *Edit Microsoft Drawing Object* from the **Edit** menu.

Follow the same procedure for returning to the Word Processor document as outlined above. This will ensure that the graphic is updated when you return to the document.

SPREADSHEET 4

INTRODUCTION

A spreadsheet is a table of columns and rows into which text, numbers, and formulas are inserted. The spreadsheet data is used to make calculations, plan budgets, and perform other mathematical tasks. A spreadsheet can also undertake "What if?" analysis to simplify and speed up the production of forecasts.

The data in the spreadsheet can then be used to create a chart, which displays the information in a graphical—and more interesting—format.

The Spreadsheet tool is opened in the same way as the other tools in Works. Many of the common features of Works, which are outlined in **Chapter 2** of this book, are relevant when using the spreadsheet. Specific Spreadsheet features are outlined in this chapter.

THE SPREADSHEET SCREEN

Figure 1. Many of the components of the spreadsheet screen will be familiar to you if you have worked with other Works tools. The Title Bar, for instance, is identical except for the file names displayed. When a new file is opened, *Sheet1* appears, informing you that a new spreadsheet or "worksheet" is on the screen. The extension of a spreadsheet file is also different—".*wks*" is used for spreadsheet files.

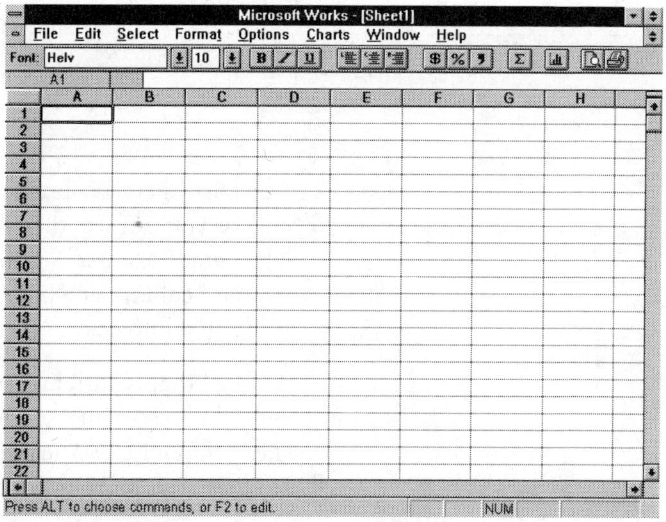

Figure 2. The menu and Toolbar options incorporate many of the Works standards. Naturally, many new commands and functions are used in the Spreadsheet tool. These will be covered in the appropriate sections of this chapter.

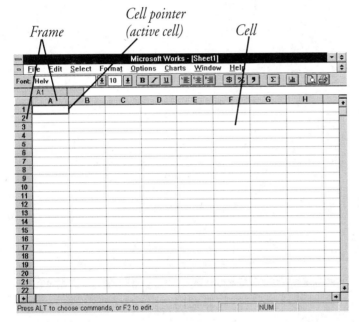

Figure 3. The worksheet screen is a table that is divided into columns and rows. The columns and rows in the worksheet are labeled logically. The rows are labeled with numbers that can be seen on the vertical "frame" on the left side of the screen. The columns are labeled with letters that appear on the horizontal frame.

The area where a column and row intersect is called a "cell" and, as you can see, there are many cells in the spreadsheet. The name of one cell—the cell address—is determined by the row and column at which it intersects—for example, D5. Data is inserted into cells in the worksheet.

The cell that is currently selected is referred to as the "active cell." This cell is marked by a darker outline, which is called the "cell pointer." The cell pointer can be moved around the worksheet to make other cells active.

Figure 4. The name of the active cell is displayed in the Formula Bar, which is just below the Menu Bar on the spreadsheet screen. The Formula Bar also contains a Cancel button (the cross) and an Enter button (the check mark). These are the mouse equivalents to pressing Esc and Enter on the keyboard.

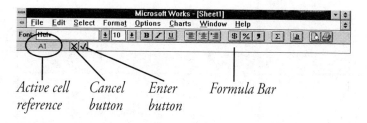

Active cell   Cancel   Enter   Formula Bar
reference   button   button

The area to the right of these buttons is used to input data. Information entered into a cell will appear in the Formula Bar when that cell is selected, as well as continuously in the cell itself. Editing the contents of a cell is done in the Formula Bar.

MOVING AROUND THE SCREEN

USING THE MOUSE

Figure 5. To move to another cell using the mouse, simply click on the cell required. If the cell you need cannot be seen on the screen, you can use the mouse to activate the scroll bars. The scroll bars operate in the same way as outlined in **Chapter 2 — Common Features.**

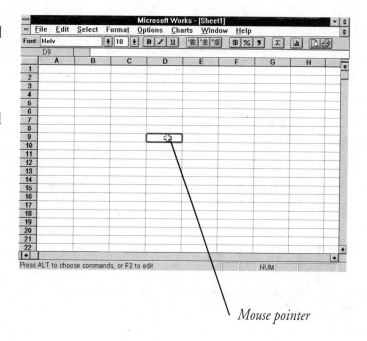

Mouse pointer

USING THE KEYBOARD

To Move	Keyboard	To Move	Keyboard
Left one cell	Left arrow or Shift Tab	Up one row	Up arrow
Right one cell	Right arrow or Tab	Down one row	Down arrow
To beginning of row	Home	To beginning of spreadsheet	Ctrl+Home
To end of row	End	To end of spreadsheet	Ctrl+End
Up one screen	Page Up	Left one screen	Ctrl+Page Up
Down one screen	Page Down	Right one screen	Control+Page Down

Figure 6. There are a number of keyboard shortcuts for moving around the worksheet quickly. These are outlined in the table displayed.

GO TO

The *Go To* command in the **Select** menu moves you to a specific cell or range of cells in the worksheet.

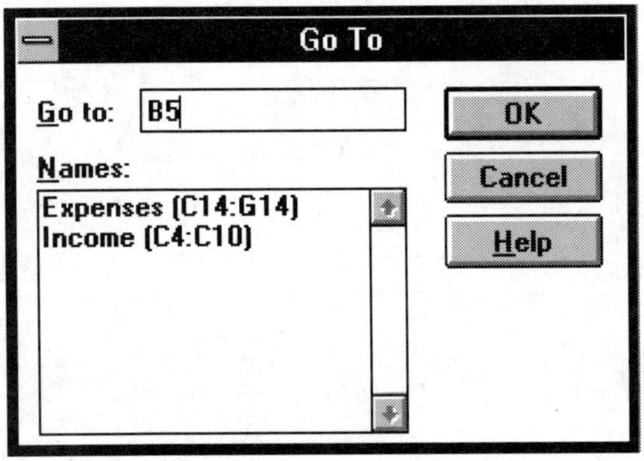

Figure 7. To use this feature, display the *Go To* dialog box by selecting the *Go To* command from the **Select** menu. The keyboard shortcut is to press F5. To move to a specific cell, key in the name of the cell in the *Go to* text box and then click on *OK*.

When Range Names—outlined later in this chapter—have been established in the worksheet, they will be listed in the *Names* list box. To move to a particular range, click on the range name and then on *OK*.

FIND

The Find feature locates a specific cell entry, such as a label or a formula. Choose *Find* from the **Select** menu to display the *Find* dialog box.

Figure 8. Works will search the spreadsheet for the characters inserted into the *Find What* text box. You can specify how the search is to be performed—by rows or columns.

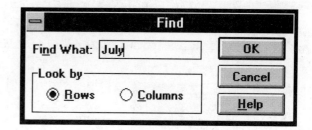

To start the search, click on *OK* and Works will search through all cells in the worksheet until the first occurrence of the text is found.

The pointer highlights the cell that contains identical characters to the contents of the *Find What* text box. The search can be repeated by pressing F7.

HIGHLIGHTING DATA

Cells must be highlighted before they can be manipulated. Once they have been highlighted, you can make changes to the spreadsheet format, the cell contents, etc. At least one cell is highlighted at any time when using a worksheet. The cell that is marked with the pointer is referred to as the highlighted or active cell.

It is often necessary to highlight more than one cell. A group of highlighted cells is called a range. Ranges can save you time when formatting and are also used widely in mathematical functions.

USING THE MOUSE

To highlight one cell with the mouse, move the mouse cursor over the cell required and click the mouse button. The pointer immediately moves to this cell and highlights it. Works also informs you by displaying the cell address in the Formula Bar.

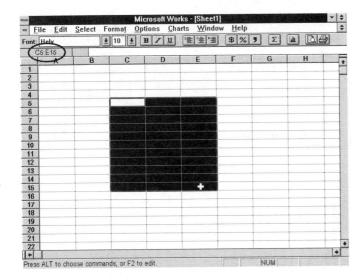

Figure 9. The click-and-drag technique is used to highlight a range of cells. Click on the first cell in the range and drag down to the last cell. When you release the mouse button, the cells will be highlighted. The cell range will appear in the Formula Bar—for example, as C5:E15.

Click here to highlight the entire spreadsheet

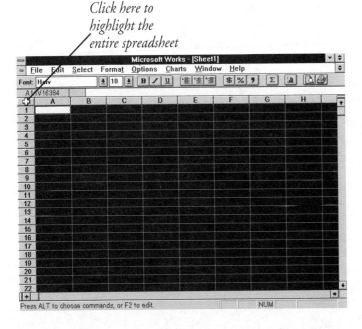

Figure 10. To highlight an entire row, click on a row label on the frame. A column is selected by clicking on a column label. The entire worksheet is selected by clicking on the frame in the top left corner of the screen.

USING THE KEYBOARD

Figure 11. The keyboard shortcuts for highlighting a cell and ranges of cells are outlined in the table illustrated.

To Highlight	Mouse	Keyboard
A cell	Click on the cell	Press arrow key to cell
A row	Click on the row number	Ctrl+F8
A column	Click on column letter	Shift+F8
A block of cells	Drag pointer over cells	F8 to extend then use arrow keys to move to cells
The entire spreadsheet	Click on button in the top left corner of frame	Ctrl+Shift+F8

USING THE SELECT MENU

Figure 12. The **Select** menu offers a number of options for selecting various combinations of cells.

Figure 13. To select ranges of cells using the **Select** menu, choose *Cells*. When this command is selected, Works displays EXT in the Status Bar. While in "extended cursor mode," either the mouse or the cursor keys will select multiple cells. To turn extended cursor mode off, press Esc.

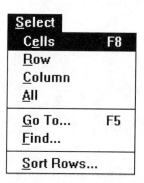

The *Column* and *Row* commands in the **Select** menu select Columns and Rows, respectively. The entire worksheet is selected by choosing *All*.

ENTERING DATA

Four types of data can be inserted into a worksheet: labels, values, formulas, and functions. Works inserts the data into the active cell. It is essential, therefore, that you move the pointer to the correct cell before inserting data of any kind.

LABELS

Labels are items of text inserted into a worksheet as column and/or row headings or as a spreadsheet title. Labels are an essential part of overall spreadsheet development, adding meaning to the figures it contains.

Enter button   *Text being entered*

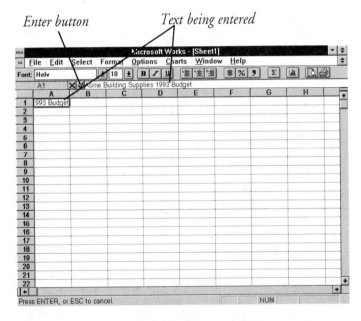

Figure 14. To insert a label, highlight the correct cell and simply key in the text to make up the label. As you are typing, the text is entered into both the cell and the Formula Bar. The text cursor appears in the Formula Bar and disappears when you press Enter or click on the Enter button. When text is "entered," it is "officially" part of the worksheet and is called the "cell contents."

Label prefix

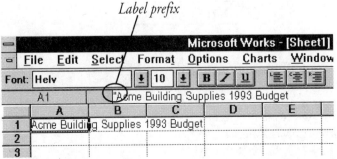

Figure 15. Works displays a label prefix in the Formula Bar as soon as a label is entered. The label prefix is a set of quotation marks that appears at the beginning of every label in the worksheet.

Figure 16. Occasionally a label will be longer than the column width. Works does not object to this and simply uses the space in any blank cell(s) to the right to display extra information if available.

A problem can arise if the cell to the right is not blank. When this happens, the cell contents will be truncated, as illustrated. This figure shows both of these scenarios.

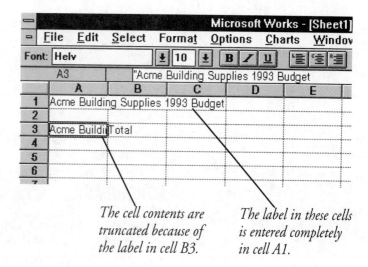

The cell contents are truncated because of the label in cell B3.

The label in these cells is entered completely in cell A1.

The actual cell contents are not altered in any way. This can be checked by looking at the text in the Formula Bar, where you can see that the entire label is still displayed.

Redisplaying the entire cell contents (in the actual cell) can be achieved only by widening the column that is outlined in the **Formatting Worksheets** section of this chapter.

VALUES

Figure 17. Values are the figures that are typed into a worksheet. The numeric keypad on your keyboard is very useful for entering numbers, although the numbers above the letters do the same thing.

Values

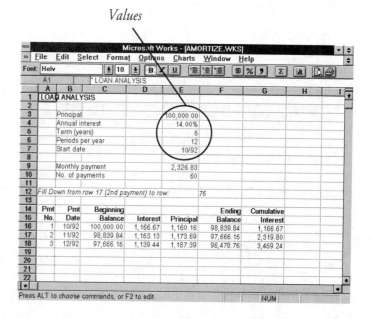

Unlike labels, which may be too long for a cell, values are never truncated but appear in one of two forms:

1. Works converts the value to scientific notation—for example, 1E+10.
2. The number is replaced with a series of hatch symbols, #########.

The actual cell contents can always be viewed in full in the Formula Bar.

FORMULAS

Formulas are equations that perform calculations on the existing values in a worksheet. The first and most important part of creating a formula is to move to the cell that is to contain the formula. Once the cell is selected, a formula prefix must be typed into the cell. The formula prefix is an equals sign (=).

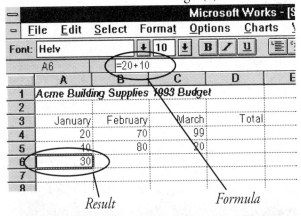

Result   *Formula*

Figure 18. Basic formulas can contain values that are added, or subtracted, etc., such as 20+10. In the Formula Bar, the formula would appear as "=20+10." In the cell, however, the answer of 30 would be displayed.

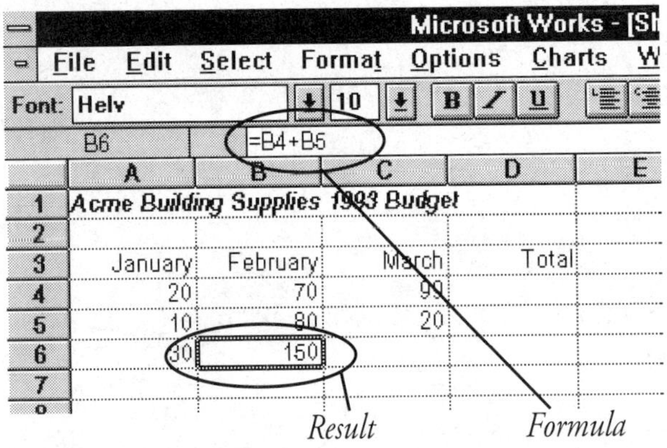

Figure 19. To use the spreadsheet data more efficiently, cell references are inserted into the formula. The example illustrated shows the formula "=B4+B5" with the answer of 150 in cell B6.

This type of formula is more flexible because the result will be automatically updated if the values in the cells are changed.

Result   *Formula*

The formula can combine any cell in the spreadsheet with any of the mathematical operators and symbols listed below:

+	addition
-	subtraction
*	multiplication
/	division
^	exponential
( )	brackets

Figure 20. To insert a formula using cell references, move to the correct cell and key in the formula prefix. You then move to the first cell required in the formula, using the mouse or the keyboard.

The next step is to insert the mathematical operator. The cell pointer then jumps back to the original cell, ready for you to move to the next cell used in the formula.

Check that the formula is displayed in the Formula Bar as it is being created.

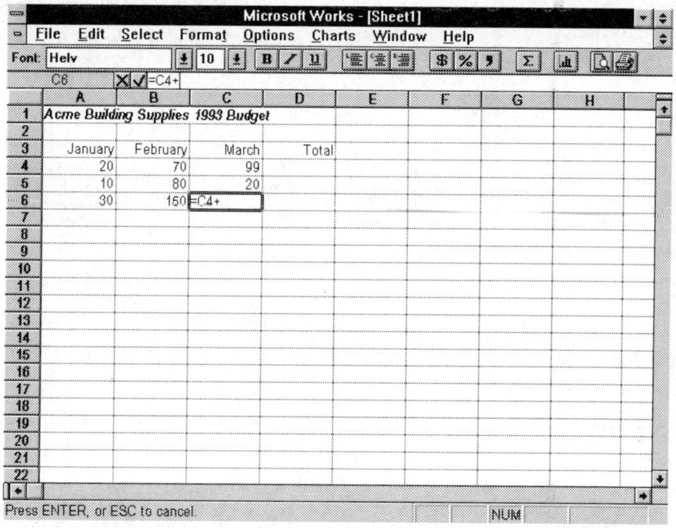

Figure 21. You can continue adding cells and operators in this way until the formula is complete. Once it is complete, press Enter to calculate the formula and obtain the total.

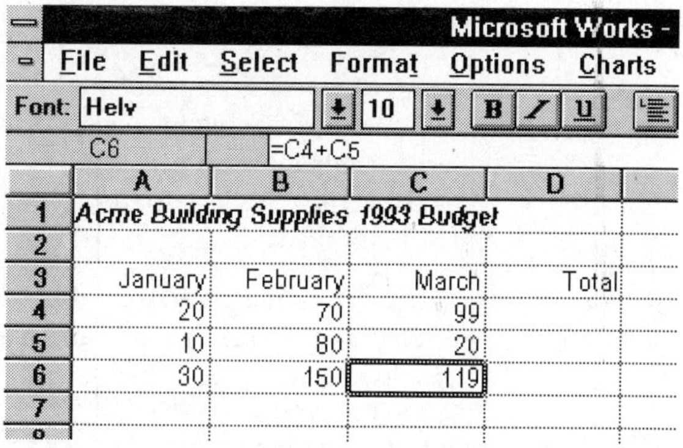

FUNCTIONS

Functions are preprogrammed mathematical equations that are part of the Works program. Fifty-seven functions are available in Works to perform various mathematical operations in a spreadsheet.

There are functions designed to add a range of cells, compute the average of a range of cells, determine the serial number of a date calculated from January 1, 1900, and check for a given condition and perform calculations depending on whether the condition is true or false, to name a few.

Functions are designed to save time by enabling you to calculate complex formulas more simply. The simplicity stems from the consistency of the formulas. Most functions apply the standard syntax of:

=FUNCTION NAME(cell references)

Figure 22. Some of the functions are listed in the table. A complete list of functions is provided in **Appendix A** of the **Microsoft Works User's Guide.**

ABS(x)	Gives the absolute (positive) value of x	LOG(x)	Gives the base 10 logarithm of x.
AVG(range)	Finds the average of a range of cells.	MIN(range)	Gives the smallest value in a range.
COUNT(range)	Counts the number of cells in the range.	NOW( )	Specifies the current date and time serial number according to the internal clock.
DATE(Year, Month, Day)	Converts the date into a serial number determined by the number of days from Jan 1, 1900.	PMT(Principal, Rate, Term)	Calculates a periodic payment for a loan or investment.
IF(Condition, If True, If False)	Tests for a condition and displays the If True data if condition is true and If False if condition is false.	ROUND(x, Number of Places)	Rounds x to the number of decimal places specified.

Figure 23. The function syntax applies to most functions. To insert a function, the formula prefix needs to be keyed in first. This is essential because it is, in fact, a type of formula.

The name of the function is inserted directly after the formula prefix; no spaces are required to separate the prefix from the function name. The name of the function can be typed in upper- or lowercase.

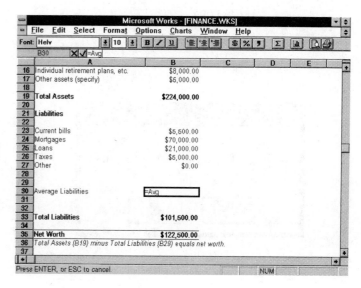

The function inserted may be AVG, for example, which calculates the average of a range of numbers.

Figure 24. Following the open parenthesis, which is inserted next, the cell address, or range of the data that is specific to the calculation being performed, is entered. The cell range can be keyed in directly, or for more accuracy, can be pointed to with the cell pointer. This is called creating a formula by "pointing."

To highlight a range using the keyboard, move to the first cell in the range and "anchor" it there by pressing the colon (:). Once it is anchored, you can highlight the cells required using this cell (the anchored cell) as a starting point. When the cells are being highlighted, "POINT" will appear in the Status Bar. To highlight with the mouse, simply swipe the cells in the cell range.

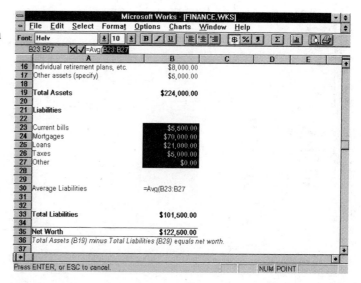

Figure 25. To complete the function, insert a right parenthesis and press Enter. Should you forget to close the parentheses, an error message will appear on the screen. Click on *OK*, add a right parenthesis, and press Enter to continue.

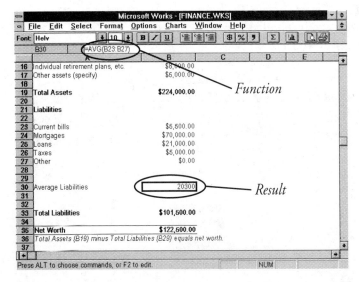

Figure 26. When the formula is complete, the function will appear in the Formula Bar and the result will appear in the cell.

AUTOSUM

Figure 27. The most widely used function is the SUM function, which adds a range of cells together. This avoids having to develop long (and tedious!) formulas such as A1+A2+A3+A4+A5+....   Because this function is used extensively in worksheet development, Works provides the *Autosum* button on the Toolbar with which to insert it.

Figure 28. To use the *Autosum* button to add a series of cells quickly, move the pointer to a blank cell at the end of the column or row of cells to be added and click on the *Autosum* button.

Autosum button

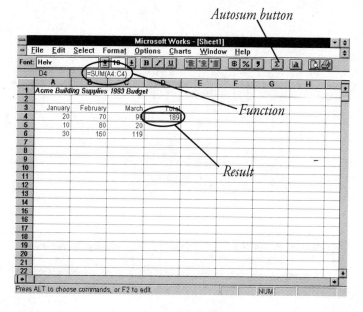

Function

Result

Works first attempts to include the cells with value entries above the active cell. If no value cells are above the active cell, it will include the cells to the left. The cells to be used in the function are highlighted, and the range reference is inserted into the Formula Bar.

Parentheses are inserted into the function automatically. To complete the function, press Enter and the cells in the range will be added together. The cell displays the result while the Formula Bar displays the function, as shown in Figure 28.

FILL COMMANDS

The *Fill Right* and *Fill Down* commands copy data to adjacent cells in the spreadsheet more quickly than the conventional copy routine. Basic cell entries can be copied as well as formats, formulas, and functions.

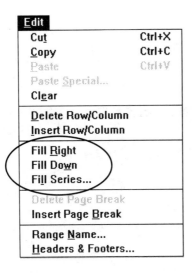

Figure 29. Works includes three Fill commands to help you to insert data into the spreadsheet quickly. The three commands are *Fill Right, Fill Down,* and *Fill Series* in the **Edit** menu.

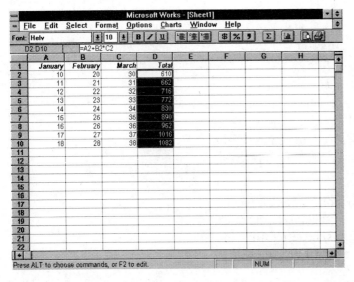

Figure 30. The cell contents to be copied are inserted into the first cell in the block before the *Fill* commands can be used. For example, a formula inserted into cell D2 may be appropriate for a number of adjacent cells. Instead of having to re-create this formula for other cells below, highlight the required cells and use the *Fill Down* command to copy the data to these cells.

Figure 31. The same principle applies to functions that are copied using the *Fill* commands. For example, to copy the Sum function in the worksheet shown, highlight the cells to which it is to be copied, including the cell that contains the function, and choose *Fill Right*.

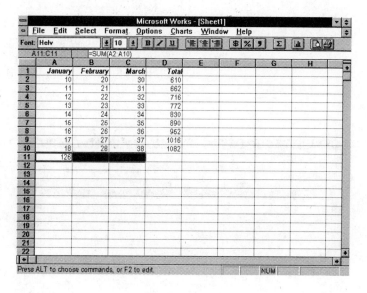

To copy formats using the *Fill* commands, ensure that the cells contain the formats only. If the cells contain any data as well as formats, the formats and the data will be inserted into the cells.

Figure 32. The *Fill Series* command in the **Edit** menu allows you to insert data—which follows a logical pattern—into a group of highlighted cells.

The types of series that can be inserted are simple number series or a date series based on the days in the week, the months, or the year.

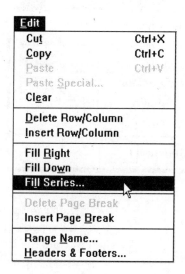

To insert a series of dates, the data must be initially inserted using the date function, then formatted with the *Time/Date* command in the **Format** menu. Figure 33 shows the example "=DATE(94,1,3)" formatted with the *Month only* date style.

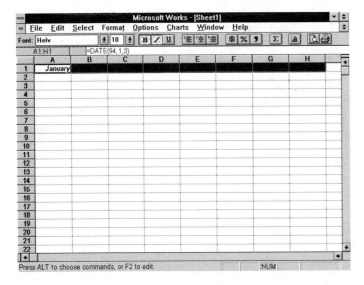

Figure 33. The first cell in the series must be inserted. Once the cells for the series are highlighted, select *Fill Series* from the **Edit** menu.

Figure 34. In the *Fill Series* dialog box, select the type units on which the series is to be based. The options available depend on the type of data inserted in the first cell. Only when a date has been inserted using the DATE function will the date units functions be offered.

The *Step by* text box specifies the increment that is to be used in the series. Any amount can be entered. A negative number decreases the series. To create the series, click on *OK.* Once inserted, the figures become part of the worksheet as values that can be edited and formatted.

EDITING WORKSHEETS

Data in many worksheets often need to be changed. Works has a number of options to help you edit your worksheet efficiently, many of which are standard features of all the Works tools. Editing features of this kind are outlined in this section.

DELETING CELLS

Figure 35. To delete the contents of a single cell, highlight the cell and press the Delete key. The cell contents are removed, but the text cursor remains in the Formula Bar ready for you to add new cell contents immediately.

Key in the cell contents that are to replace what was deleted, or press Enter to clear the cell completely and return to the worksheet.

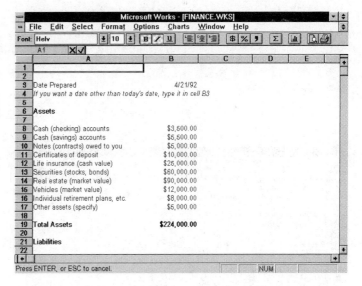

Figure 36. Using the Delete key to delete a number of cells would be too time consuming to be practical. The *Clear* command in the **Edit** menu is designed for this purpose.

To delete an entire range of cells, highlight the cells to be deleted and choose *Clear* from the **Edit** menu. The cell contents of those highlighted cells are removed, but the formatting remains.

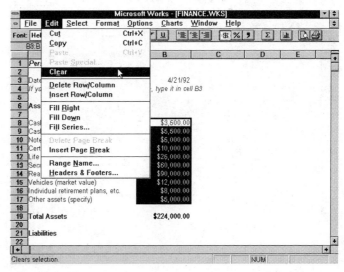

CUTTING, COPYING, AND PASTING

The Cut, Copy, and Paste facilities are used in the same way as outlined in **Chapter 2 — Common Features.** When a cell is *Cut,* it is completely removed from the original position, only appearing in the worksheet again when it is reinserted using the *Paste* command. The *Copy* command, in conjunction with the *Paste* command, allows you to obtain more than one copy of an original cell in the worksheet.

Using these commands to manipulate labels and values is straightforward. Working with formulas, however, is not so straightforward and is outlined in this section.

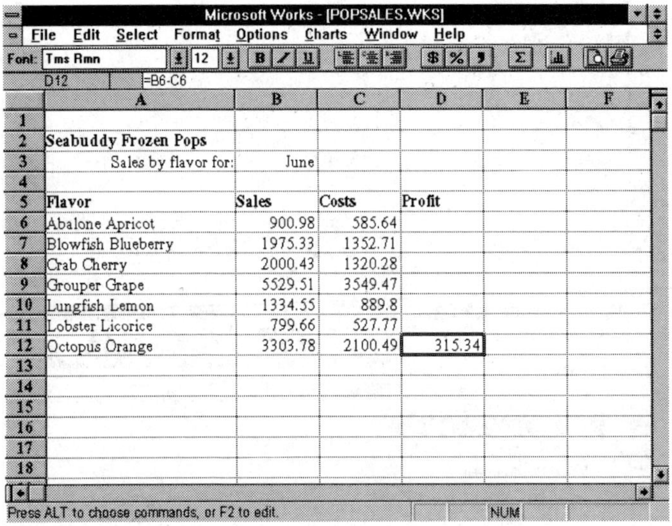

Figure 37. Formulas pasted in a worksheet after being *Cut* retain exactly the same formula as contained in the original cell.

In this figure, the formula in cell D6 has been cut and then pasted into D12. The formula still subtracts C6 from B6 to calculate the profit from the sale of Abalone Apricot.

This formula no longer corresponds to the row into which it has been pasted. It is important to remember this when using the *Cut* command with formulas.

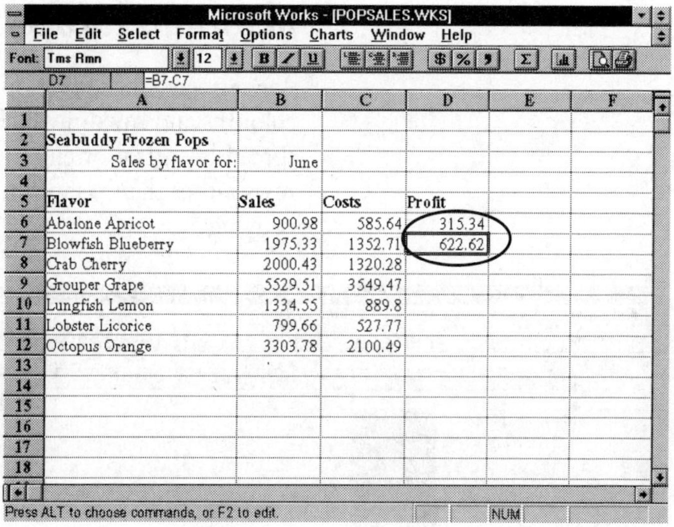

Figure 38. A formula that is copied into a new cell will be copied relatively. Copying relatively means that the formula retains the same basic form but adjusts the cell references in the formula in relation to its new position in the worksheet.

In this figure, the formula "=B6-C6" was copied from D6 to D7. In that cell it now calculates the formula "=B7-C7" in cell D7, which is correct.

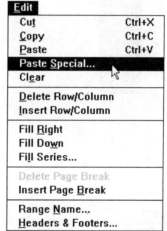

Figure 39. The other feature of the spreadsheet tool to keep in mind when cutting and copying is the *Paste Special* command in the **Edit** menu.

This command performs a number of special tasks that are particularly useful when summarizing worksheet data.

Figure 40. The *Paste Special* options are:

- Pasting the result *only* of a formula in a new location
- Adding the result of a cut or copied formula to the highlighted cell
- Subtracting the result of a cut or copied formula to the highlighted cell

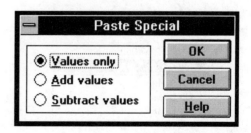

INSERTING COLUMNS AND ROWS

As your worksheet develops, it is often necessary to add new columns and rows in which to enter data to update the spreadsheet. It is often much easier to add extra columns and rows rather than reshuffling the spreadsheet by cutting and copying.

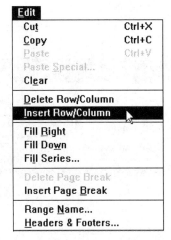

	A	B	C	D	E	F
1						
2	Seabuddy Frozen Pops					
3	Sales by flavor for:	June				
4						
5	Flavor	Sales	Costs	Profit		
6	Abalone Apricot	900.98	585.64	315.34		
7	Blowfish Blueberry	1975.33	1352.71	622.62		
8	Crab Cherry	2000.43	1320.28	680.15		
9	Grouper Grape	5529.51	3549.47	1980.04		
10	Lungfish Lemon	1334.55	889.8	444.75		
11	Lobster Licorice	799.66	527.77	271.89		
12	Octopus Orange	3303.78	2100.49	1203.29		

Figure 41. The position of the cursor is important when inserting new columns and rows. To insert a row in a particular place in the worksheet, highlight the row where the new row is to be inserted.

In a similar fashion, the column where the new column is to be inserted should be highlighted first. In this figure, column B is highlighted and therefore a new column will be inserted to the left of column B.

New rows/columns are added above or to the left of the highlighted row or column, respectively.

Edit menu:

Cut	Ctrl+X
Copy	Ctrl+C
Paste	Ctrl+V
Paste Special...	
Clear	
Delete Row/Column	
Insert Row/Column	
Fill Right	
Fill Down	
Fill Series...	
Delete Page Break	
Insert Page Break	
Range Name...	
Headers & Footers...	

Figure 42. To insert the new row or column, select *Insert Row/Column* from the **Edit** menu. Works will automatically place a new blank row or column in the appropriate position, depending on whether a column or row was selected.

Figure 43. If a row or column is not selected before the *Insert Row/Column* command is selected, the *Insert* dialog box appears. In this dialog box, you can choose whether to insert a row or column, which will be placed at the cursor position.

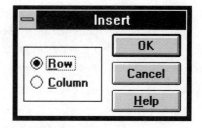

Deleting rows and columns is also a very important part of spreadsheet editing. You will need to delete blank rows and columns as well as those with data in them. Works, however, makes no distinction between blank or used rows and columns. It simply deletes them with no warning—so make certain that you will not be losing anything important before you activate this command!

Figure 44. Rows and columns are deleted in the same way as they are inserted. If a row or a column is highlighted, then it will be removed from the worksheet when *Delete Row/Column* is selected. When only a single cell is selected, the *Delete* dialog box appears, asking you to choose whether to delete the row or the column.

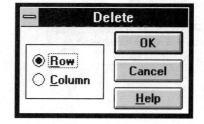

RECALCULATION

There are two types of calculation that can be applied to the worksheet: *manual* and *automatic*. Automatic is the default setting and, when active, recalculates the spreadsheet automatically whenever any changes are made. Having recalculation active ensures that the worksheet is always displayed in the most up-to-date form.

Although this sounds ideal, there are times when automatic recalculation can become a burden. When your worksheet is large and contains many complex formulas and intricate formatting, for instance, it can take considerable time to recalculate.

If you don't want to wait for the worksheet to recalculate each time you make a change, choose the manual recalculation mode.

Figure 45. To change the mode of recalculation to manual, choose *Manual Calculation* from the **Options** menu.

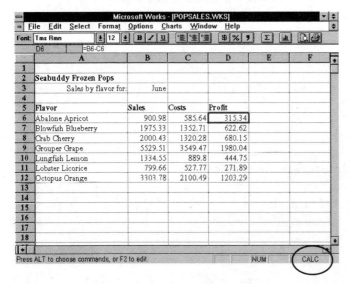

Figure 46. When Manual Calculation is active, "CALC" appears in the Status Bar as a mode indicator. This warns you that your worksheet may not be displaying accurate results of formulas, because changes may have been made since the spreadsheet was last recalculated.

Figure 47. To update the worksheet, choose *Calculate Now* from the **Options** menu or press F9 as the keyboard shortcut.

```
Options
    Works Settings...
    Dial This Number

 √ Show Toolbar
 √ Show Gridlines
    Show Formulas
    Freeze Titles
    Protect Data

 √ Manual Calculation
    Calculate Now      F9
```

FORMATTING WORKSHEETS

As well as accuracy in calculation, the presentation of your worksheet is an essential part of spreadsheet development. Formatting can be used not only to grab the attention of readers, but also to highlight specific sections of the worksheet and generally make it more attractive and easier to read and comprehend.

NUMERIC FORMATS

Figure 48. Because a spreadsheet deals specifically with figures, it is essential to be able to manipulate the appearance of these figures easily. This process is referred to as changing the numeric format of a value. This can be done either by using the **Format** menu for a comprehensive list of options, or the Toolbar, for applying the most common of those options—*Currency, Percent,* and *Comma.*

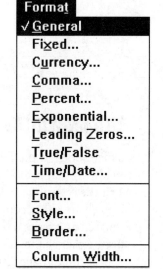

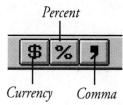

General	1234.56
Fixed	1234.56
Currency	$1,234.56
Comma	1,234.56
Percent	123456.00%
Exponential	1.23E+03
Leading Zeros	001235
True/False	TRUE
Time/Date	5/18/95

Figure 49. This table lists the numeric formats available, including examples of currency, percentage, and comma—the three buttons accessible through the Toolbar.

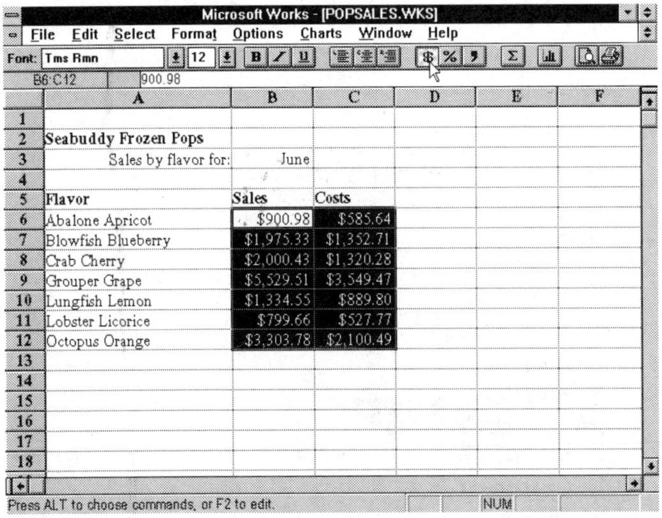

Figure 50. To change the format of a value already inserted into the worksheet, highlight the cell, or range of cells, and choose the format required from the **Format** menu or the Toolbar. Numeric formats can also be set before a value is keyed into the worksheet. To do this, select the format required and then the value.

COLUMN WIDTHS

As mentioned in the **Entering Data** section of this chapter, a label (text) that is too long to display in a cell can be truncated when the cell to the right is not blank. Values that are too long for a cell are either converted to scientific notation, or displayed as a series of hatch symbols. Column widths often must be changed to display cell contents more clearly. Column widths can be changed in two ways: by using the mouse or using the keyboard.

USING THE MOUSE

Figure 51. When the cursor is placed near a column separator, it changes shape. This cursor shape allows you to adjust column widths. The column separators on the frame are dragged to the left or the right when you alter the column widths using the mouse. This is a quick and easy way of changing the width of a column.

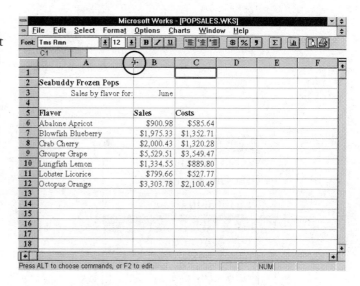

USING THE KEYBOARD

Figure 52. To set the width of a column exactly, choose the *Column Width* command from the **Format** menu and key in the exact width of the column in the *Width* text box.

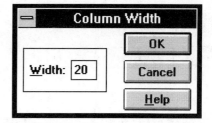

When you click on *OK*, the column in which the pointer is located will change to the width specified. To change the width of more than one column at one time, highlight the columns—or just some cells in those columns—and repeat the process of changing the width of one column.

BORDERS

Borders are used to attract attention to specific cells in the spreadsheet. Borders using a specific style can be designated to a cell or a range of cells.

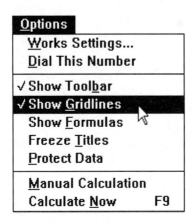

Figure 53. It is often difficult to see the inserted borders when the gridlines are displayed in the worksheet. To turn gridlines off, deselect *Show Gridlines* from the **Options** menu.

Figure 54. Borders are added to the worksheet by selecting the *Border* command in the **Format** menu. This displays the *Border* dialog box in which you select the type of border—*Outline, Top, Bottom, Left,* and/or *Right.*

SORTING

Data inserted into a spreadsheet randomly can be sorted numerically or alphabetically in ascending or descending order. The *Sort Rows* command in the **Select** menu is used for this purpose.

Works can sort one, two, or three columns at once. A three level sort, for example, could arrange a list of employees in alphabetical order by department, then alphabetical order by names, and finally numeric order by salary.

Figure 55. The data to be sorted must be selected first. If not all the data is selected, the spreadsheet will not end up in any logical order.

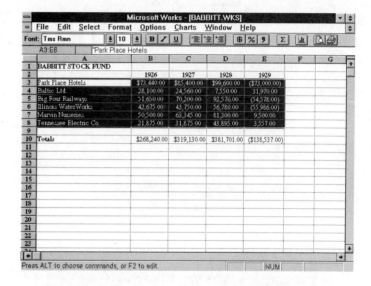

Figure 56. In the *Sort Rows* dialog box, specify how the sort is to be ordered and click on *OK* to arrange the data appropriately. In this figure, the data in column A will be sorted in ascending order.

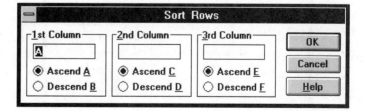

RANGE NAMES

Ranges are used in spreadsheet functions and formulas, and when editing. Often, you must constantly refer to the same range of cells. Works provides the *Range Name* feature, which makes this task easier by giving the range a name, which is much easier to remember than cell references.

Once in place, range names can be used in calculations and with the *Go To* command.

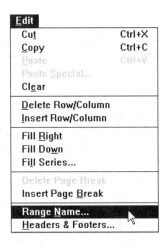

Figure 57. To insert a range name, highlight the range of cells to be named and select *Range Name* from the **Edit** menu.

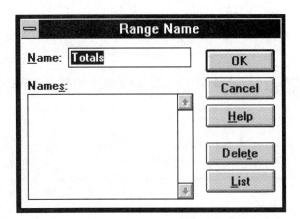

Figure 58. The name of the range is specified in the *Name* text box. If the type of information in the range is text, the data in the first cell of the range is inserted in the *Name* text box automatically. If a range of values is selected and there is a label above the values, this label will be inserted into the *Name* text box. If nothing appears, or you want to change the name, type in the name you like and click on *OK*.

Figure 59. When a number of range names have been added to the worksheet, they are listed in the *Names* list box in the *Range Name* dialog box.

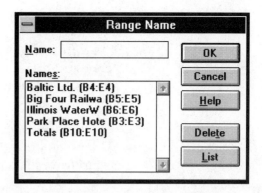

Figure 60. Range names can be used instead of cell references in functions and formulas.

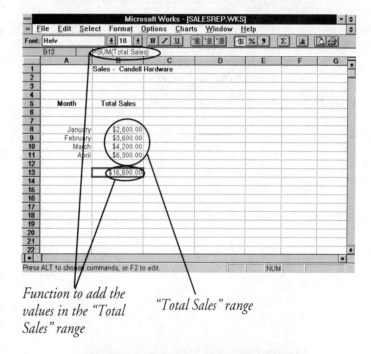

Function to add the values in the "Total Sales" range

"Total Sales" range

Figure 61. You can also use the *Go To* command to highlight the range quickly by selecting it from the *Names* list box in the *Go To* dialog box.

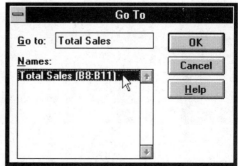

CHARTS

Charts are created in Works for the graphic representation of spreadsheet data. Charts enable you to gain insight into the worksheet in a more interesting way than having to analyze pages of figures.

The charting facilities in Works are quite powerful. Options allow you to specify cell references for data series, use colors and patterns, and format text and styles of titles.

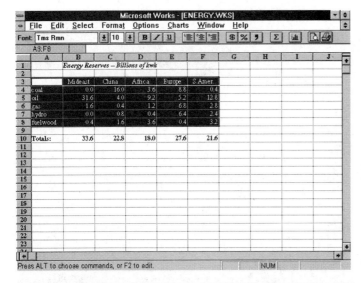

CREATING CHARTS

Figure 62. The first step in creating a chart is to decide what the chart is to represent. Once this is determined, highlight the cells that will enable you to create the chart. The highlighted cells can include labels, values, and formulas.

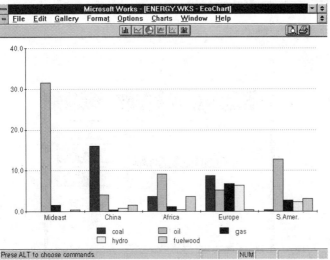

Figure 63. A new chart is created by selecting *Create New Chart* from the **Charts** menu. The values and results of the formulas in the highlighted cells are used as the chart's data series. Each chart can contain up to six data series, represented by bars, lines, or areas, depending on the chart type selected.

Cell entries that contain text become part of the chart as X-axis series—labels on the X-axis—and as legends. All the chart components, including the data series cell references, can be edited once the basic chart is created.

FORMATTING CHARTS

A formatted chart represents the data in a different way from what was originally set. Formatting the chart in this way often makes it easier to read or enables one piece of information to stand out in the chart.

CHART TYPES

Figure 64. There are six main chart types available in Works: Bar—which is the default—Line, Pie, Stacked Line, X-Y (Scatter) charts, and Combination. To change the type of chart, you can either click on the appropriate button on the Toolbar, or select the name of the chart type from the **Gallery** menu.

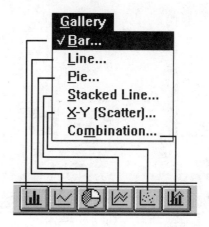

Figure 65. Each of these charts offers various style options. The options shown are part of the *Stacked Line* type of chart. Click on the style you want to use and then on *OK* to change the chart type.

The *Next* and *Previous* buttons enable you to scroll through the various chart types without having to open the dialog box for each type.

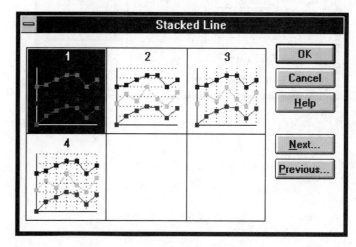

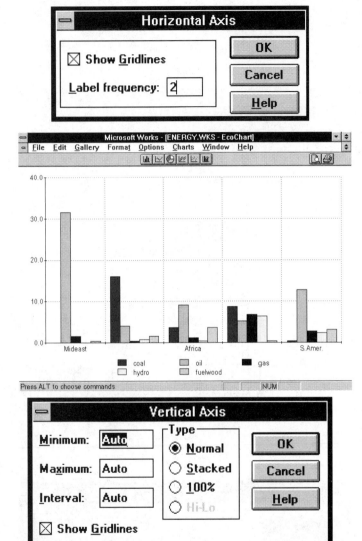

AXES

Figure 66. The horizontal axis in the chart is called the X-axis. This can be formatted in the *Horizontal Axis* dialog box, which is displayed by selecting the *Horizontal [X] axis* command in the **Format** menu. Using this dialog box, you can add vertical gridlines to the chart.

The frequency of the labels on the X-axis can also be adjusted. A frequency of two, for example, would display every second label on the X-axis. This is used to stop the labels from overlapping. The chart displayed is based on the options selected in the *Horizontal Axis* dialog box, above. (The horizontal gridlines are set using the *Vertical Axis* dialog box, discussed below.)

Figure 67. The *Vertical Axis* dialog box is displayed by selecting the *Vertical [Y] Axis* command in the **Format** menu. The main purpose of the Vertical Axis dialog box is to set the scale on the Y-axis. The maximum and minimum numbers on the scale are set by changing these text boxes from *Auto*. The intervals in the scale are changed by keying in a number in the *Interval* text box. If a *Logarithmic Scale* is required, select this option and click on *OK*. This dialog box can also change the type of vertical axis scale, as well as add horizontal gridlines.

Figure 68. A right vertical axis can be added to a chart to emphasize one particular data series in that chart. It is added by selecting *Two Vertical [Y] Axes* from the **Format** menu. In the dialog box that appears, select *Right* for the data series required. In this example, we are selecting *Right* for the *5th Value Series*.

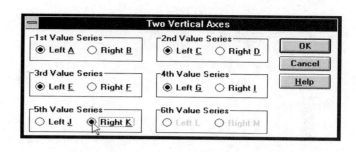

Figure 69. When you return to the chart, it will appear similar to the example shown. This axis can be formatted further using the *Right Vertical Axis* command in the **Format** menu.

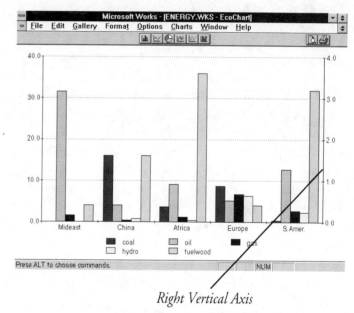

Right Vertical Axis

Figure 70. To add emphasis to a particular series in the chart, you can create a Mixed Line and Bar chart. This will display one or more of the series in a line or bar format to distinguish it from the other series in the chart.

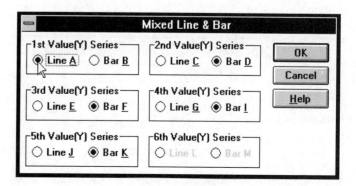

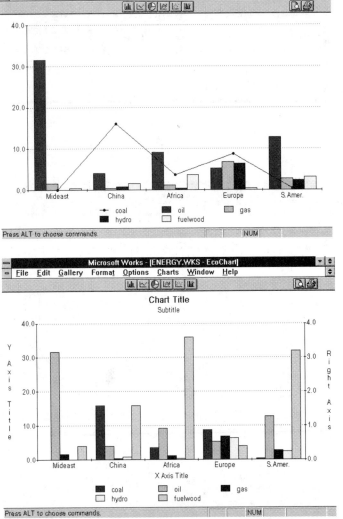

Figure 71. A mixed chart is created by selecting *Mixed Line & Bar* from the **Format** menu to activate the dialog box in Figure 70. The series in which *Line* is selected (in Figure 70, the 1st Value(y) Series) will display a line on the chart instead of a bar. The legend is automatically updated to reflect this change.

TITLES

Figure 72. Titles are an essential part of a chart because they inform you of basic chart information in words. Titles can be added to various parts of the chart. Some examples are illustrated; compare this figure with the one above.

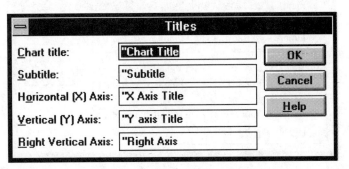

Figure 73. Chart titles are inserted by entering text in the appropriate text boxes in the *Titles* dialog box. To display the *Titles* dialog box, select *Titles* from the **Edit** menu. The text entered here represents the various title information displayed in Figure 72, above.

The different title text can be formatted using the *Title Font* and *Other Font* commands in the **Format** menu. As the names suggest, the *Title Font* command affects the chart title only, and *Other Font* affects the fonts of all other titles in the chart.

Figure 74. The options available in both of these dialog boxes are identical, enabling you to change the font, the font size, and the style.

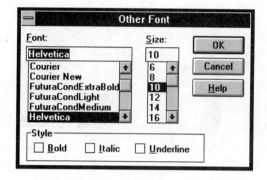

PATTERNS AND COLORS

The colors and patterns that appear in a chart when it is created are the default colors set by Works. These can be changed in the *Patterns & Colors* dialog box, which appears when the *Patterns & Colors* command is selected from the **Format** menu.

Figure 75. The series to be formatted must be selected from the *Series* section before any of its attributes can be changed. The *Colors* list box shows all the colors available to you. *Auto* resets the color back to the default. The options in the *Patterns* list box will affect different chart types in different ways. For example, a *Dotted* option under *Patterns* will only appear and affect a series that is represented by a line.

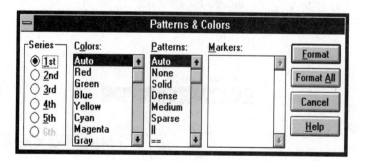

The *Markers* option affects the markers on a line that are used to separate series in a line chart.

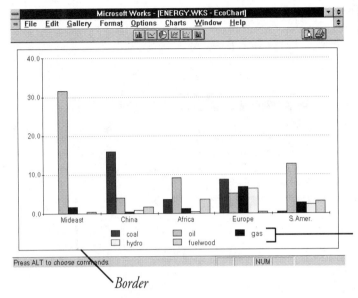

BORDER

Figure 76. You can add a border to a chart by selecting the *Show Border* option in the **Format** menu.

Border

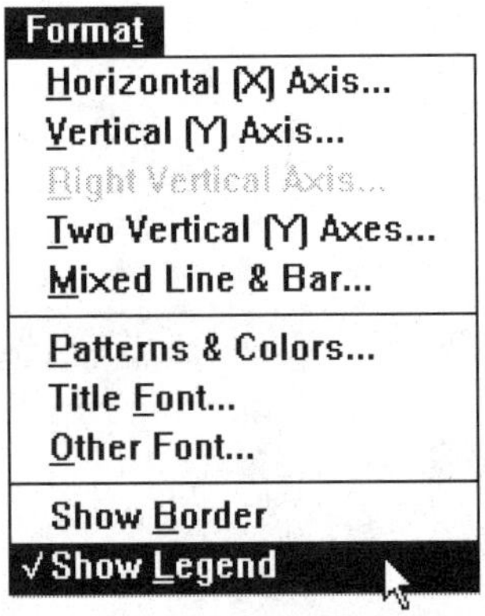

LEGENDS

Figure 77. Works automatically creates a legend using highlighted text cells in the worksheet. The legend (indicated in Figure 76) is displayed by default and can be turned off by deselecting the *Show Legend* option in the **Format** menu.

USING MULTIPLE CHARTS

Often you need to create a number of charts to represent different parts of the spreadsheet. Additional charts are created in the same way as the initial chart—simply highlight the information to be used and select *Create New Chart* from the **Charts** menu.

Works names these charts Chart1, Chart2, etc., according to the order in which they are created. A list of these charts appears at the bottom of the **Charts** menu.

SWITCHING

Figure 78. If a chart is currently displayed on screen, it will have a check mark next to it in the **Charts** menu. To display another chart in the list, choose the one you want to see from the **Charts** menu.

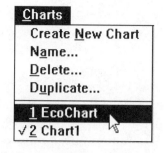

Figure 79. To return to the spreadsheet, choose the name of the spreadsheet from the **Window** menu.

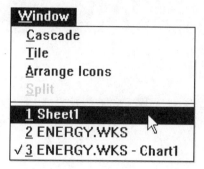

NAMING

It is often hard to distinguish between charts in the **Charts** menu using the Works naming conventions. You can give more meaningful names to a chart using the *Name Chart* dialog box. This dialog box is displayed when you select *Name* from the **Charts** menu.

Figure 80. To rename a chart, select the chart to be renamed from the *Charts* list box. Click the text cursor in the *Name* text box and key in the new name. To connect the name to the chart, click on the *Rename* button before clicking on *OK*.

The new name of the chart will then appear in the **Charts** menu.

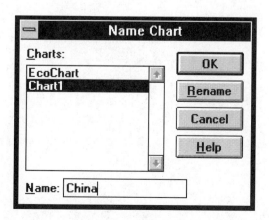

THE DATABASE 5

INTRODUCTION

The Database tool enables you to create a database file in which a collection of information can be stored and manipulated to your advantage. Whether you are creating a database from scratch, or using one that has already been developed, it is important to understand the basic structure that underlies all databases.

The database structure is made up of single pieces of information called "fields." A field can be a name or a phone number. Fields are grouped together into "records." One record contains a complete set of fields. A complete set of records is referred to as the database "file."

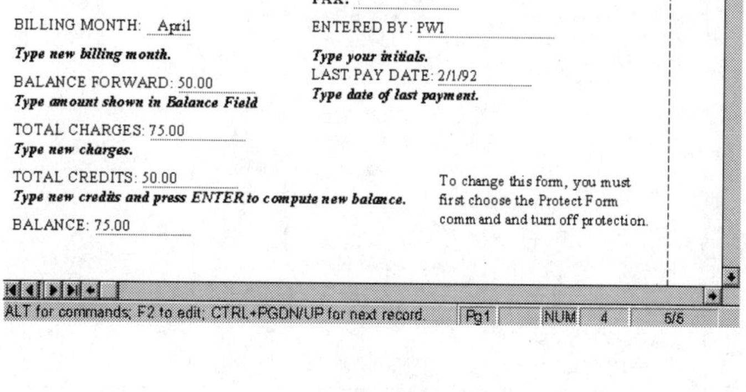

Figure 1. A database file may contain a list of client information. The database would have specific information about each client, including such things as their name, phone number, and perhaps how much they owe the company!

The database structure is beginning to take shape—each client has a record, which is made up of fields for the name, phone number, debt, etc.

This chapter will show you how to create a database and then how to use Works to manipulate the data.

THE SCREEN

The database screen incorporates many of the features found in the other Works tools, including the Title Bar, Menu Bar, scroll bars, and Toolbar. These contain some elements that are designed specifically for the database; they will be covered in the appropriate sections.

The database editing screens differ significantly from the other tools. The database uses two main screens or "views"—*List* view and *Form* view. Both are used in database development.

LIST AND FORM VIEW

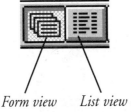

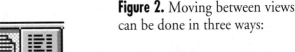

Form view   *List view*

Figure 2. Moving between views can be done in three ways:

1. Press F9.
2. Click on the appropriate button on the Toolbar.
3. Choose the view required from the **View** menu.

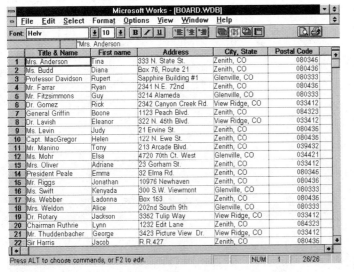

Figure 3. The List view screen is very similar to the spreadsheet one. It displays many records simultaneously; field names appear on the horizontal frame and record numbers appear on the vertical axis.

Figure 4. In Form view, only one record appears on the screen at a time, displaying all fields relating to this record. In some databases, a form is designed as an invoice sheet to be printed and sent out to individual clients.

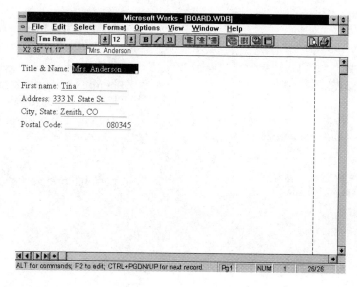

THE STATUS BAR

The Status Bar in the database shows standard information that appears in each Works tool. It also contains information that relates to records.

Figure 5. The figure to the left represents the number of the record that is currently on screen in Form view. In List view, this number is determined from the position of the pointer.

The double figures, for example "15/20," inform you that only fifteen records out of a possible twenty are currently displayed. This indicator is particularly significant when you are sorting the data or applying a query in the database.

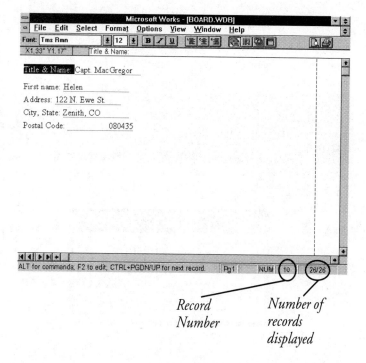

Record Number

Number of records displayed

CREATING A DATABASE

Field names are inserted in the database first of all. Before creating the database, decide on the structure you are going to follow. A little planning at this stage can save hours of time and frustration later!

The database can be created in List or Form view—or both. The view that you choose depends on your personal preference and the style of the database.

ADDING FIELDS

FORM VIEW

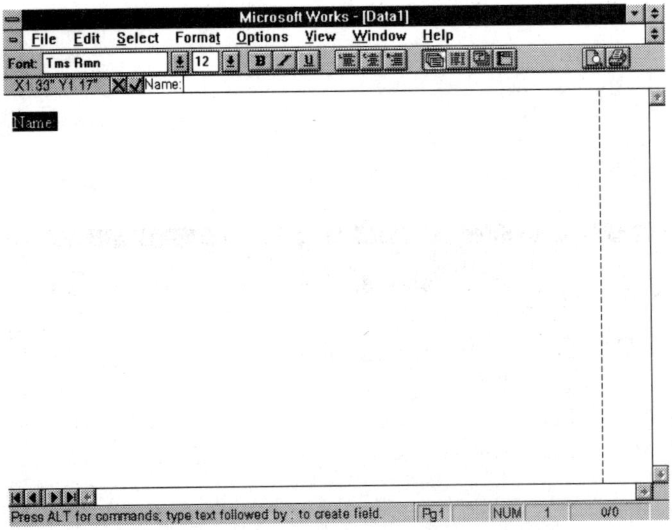

Figure 6. To insert a field in Form view, click the mouse cursor on the screen where you wish to insert the field. This positions the flashing text cursor for you to key in the field name. As you type, text appears on the editing screen as well as in the Formula Bar.

The field name must be followed by a colon (:), which is used by Works to distinguish between a field name and a comment. After the colon, press Enter. The *Field Size* dialog box then appears on the screen.

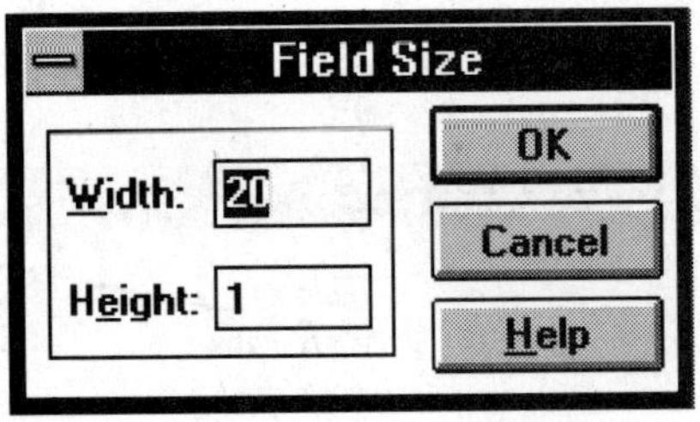

Figure 7. The *Width* of the field specifies the length of the line that will follow the field name. The *Height* determines the number of those lines that will appear. A standard field name uses a width of 20 and a height of 1.

Figure 8. Comments are used in Form view to add extra information to the form. Comments are added in the same way that fields are, except that no colon is inserted at the end of the text.

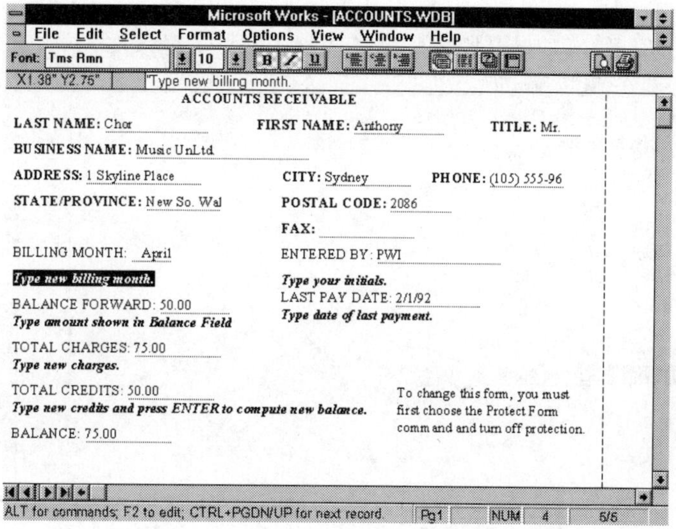

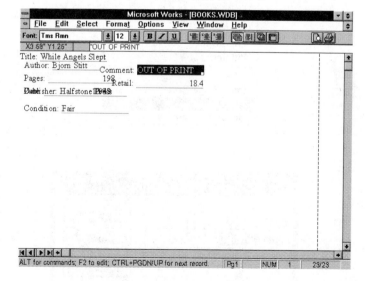

The inserted text is placed on the Form view screen and can be edited and formatted in the same way as other text covered later in this chapter. Comments do not appear in the List view screen.

Figure 9. The field names and comments can be physically reorganized to adjust the layout of the form. This is sometimes necessary when extra field names are added. Also, field names that are inserted in List view are jumbled together when you return to Form view.

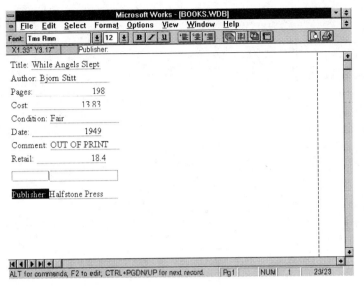

Figure 10. Field names can be moved to a new position by clicking and dragging them with the mouse. While the field name is being dragged, a small hand appears in a frame the shape of the field name. When the mouse button is released, the hand disappears and the field name moves to the new position in the form.

LIST VIEW

Figure 11. To insert a field in List view (see the screen in Figure 3), position the cursor in the correct column and select *Field Name* from the **Edit** menu.

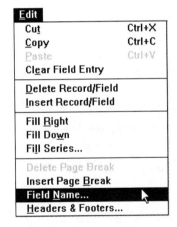

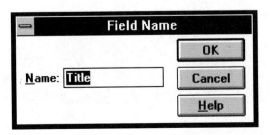

Figure 12. The field name, which can be up to fifteen characters long, is keyed into the *Name* text box in the *Field Name* dialog box. When you click on *OK*, the name of the field becomes the label heading for the column.

Figure 13. It is sometimes necessary to add a field name to the database between existing fields. A column must be inserted before the new field can be added. Use the *Insert Record/Field* command from the **Edit** menu to add the new column to the left of the current cursor position.

Edit	
Cut	Ctrl+X
Copy	Ctrl+C
Paste	Ctrl+V
Clear Field Entry	
Delete Record/Field	
Insert Record/Field	
Fill Right	
Fill Down	
Fill Series...	
Delete Page Break	
Insert Page Break	
Field Name...	
Headers & Footers...	

When this command is selected, the *Insert* dialog box appears. Choose *Field* and then *OK.* The columns at the cursor position and to its right will be pushed one column to the right, making space for a new field name to be inserted. The field name can then be added by typing it into the *Field Name* dialog box.

If you select a full column (field) before selecting this command, the new field is automatically inserted without activating the *Insert* dialog box.

ENTERING DATA

Four types of data can be inserted into a field—text, values, formulas, and functions. To add any type of information into a field, the field must be selected.

TEXT

Text is inserted as field entries by simply typing in the text required. When you press Enter, Works adds quotation marks as a text prefix. Text is automatically left aligned. Changing the alignment of cells is covered in the **Formatting** section of this chapter.

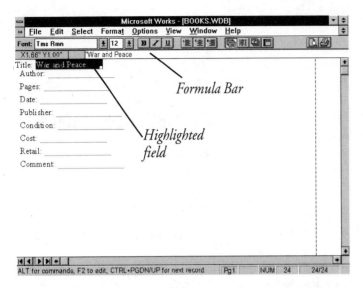

Figure 14. A field is selected in Form view by clicking on the line to the right of the field name; the highlighted field then appears as a black box.

The field entry can then be keyed in immediately after the field is highlighted. The entry is shown in the Formula Bar and the field entry area as it is being typed. When complete, press Enter.

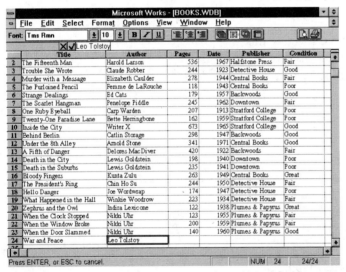

Figure 15. Field entries are added in List view in much the same way. The first step is to highlight the cell in which the entry is to be inserted and begin to type. As in Form view, the Formula Bar displays the data as it is entered. When Enter is pressed, the text becomes the field entry.

There is no limit to the length of a text field entry. When the text exceeds the designated field width, the text is truncated on the editing screen. However, the entire entry is displayed in the Formula Bar.

When the database is printed, only what appears in the field entry area will be printed. To make sure all the data in the fields is printed, extend the field entry area using a method outlined in the **Editing the Database** section later in this chapter.

VALUES

Figure 16. Values can be keyed into the field entry in the same way as text. By default, values are aligned to the right of the field and, once again, can be reformatted if required.

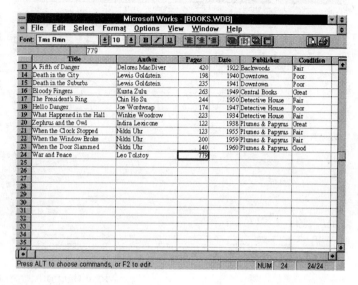

As in the spreadsheet tool, Works classifies a value as a number with a particular value, which can be used to perform calculations in functions and formulas. To use a number as a label—which has a value of zero—key in the text prefix (") before the number.

FORMULAS

Formulas are used in a database to perform calculations using values in various fields. A formula can be inserted in the database in either List or Form view. It is easier and more efficient to create the formula in List view, because in Form view a formula cannot be created by pointing to the fields required. It is also easier to copy a formula in List view.

The formula must start with an equals sign (=) as the formula prefix. You can then refer to fields within the database, for example,

"=Balance Forward+Total Charges-Total Credits"

could be used to calculate the result in a "Balance" field.

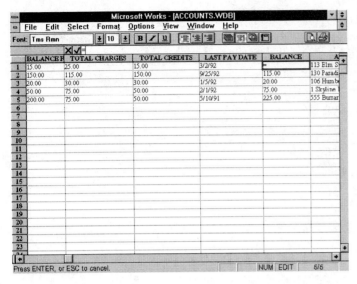

Figure 17. To insert a formula by pointing, insert the formula prefix (=) in the correct field. This is essential—otherwise the result will not appear in the correct field.

Move the pointer to the first field in the formula (by mouse or keyboard) and press the mathematical operator required. These are the same as the ones used in the spreadsheet tool:

+ addition
- subtraction
/ division
* multiplication
^ exponential
( ) parentheses

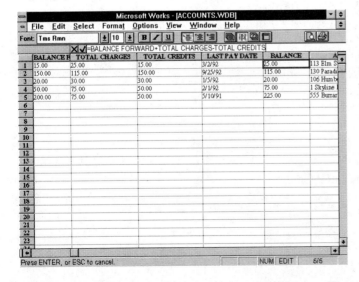

Figure 18. When the mathematical operator is keyed into the Formula Bar, the pointer immediately jumps back to the original cell. From this point, you continue pointing to the other fields required, keying in the operators as you are developing the formula.

Figure 19. When the formula is complete, check it in the Formula Bar and then press Enter. Pressing Enter calculates the result and displays it as the field entry. The actual formula is shown in the Formula Bar when the field entry is highlighted.

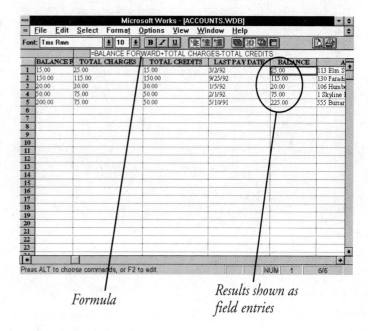

Formula

Results shown as field entries

When a formula is entered, it appears in that field in every record in the database. If a result of zero appears, it may mean that field entries have not been inserted into the fields to which the formula refers.

A formula can also be used in the database to enter the same information—text or values—into fields automatically. The information entered in this way is usually standard in every record and not likely to be changed in other records in the database. Such information may include a country, state, city, zip, or telephone area code reference.

Adding information in this way is less time consuming, often more accurate, and definitely less tedious.

	Date	Publisher	Condition	Cost	Retail	Comment	Status
1	1949	Halfstone Press	Fair	13.83	18.4	OUT OF PRINT	In Stock
2	1967	Halfstone Press	Fair	16.43	21.9	OUT OF PRINT	In Stock
3	1923	Detective House	Good	13.83	18.4		In Stock
4	1944	Central Books	Fair	16.43	22.0		In Stock
5	1943	Central Books	Poor	10.92	15.6	OUT OF PRINT	In Stock
6	1957	Backwoods	Good	10.99	13.4		In Stock
7	1962	Downtown	Fair	4.50	10.7		In Stock
8	1913	Stratford College	Poor	15.60	26.0		In Stock
9	1959	Stratford College	Poor	20.00	31.8	OUT OF PRINT	In Stock
10	1965	Stratford College	Good	15.00	17.6		In Stock
11	1947	Backwoods	Good	11.50	15.3	OUT OF PRINT	In Stock
12	1971	Central Books	Good	12.77	15.4		In Stock
13	1922	Backwoods	Fair	12.63	17.9		In Stock
14	1940	Downtown	Poor	9.00	15.0	OUT OF PRINT	In Stock
15	1941	Downtown	Poor	9.50	15.0		In Stock
16	1949	Central Books	Great	33.00	50.9	OUT OF PRINT	In Stock
17	1950	Detective House	Fair	20.00	30.0		In Stock
18	1947	Detective House	Poor	13.54	21.9		In Stock
19	1934	Detective House	Fair	12.44	15.3	OUT OF PRINT	In Stock
20	1938	Plumes & Papyrus	Great	13.99	20.0		In Stock
21	1955	Plumes & Papyrus	Fair	14.98	19.5		In Stock
22	1959	Plumes & Papyrus	Fair	15.98	21.3		In Stock
23	1960	Plumes & Papyrus	Good	14.98	19.5		In Stock

Figure 20. Adding this type of formula follows the same procedure as entering a normal formula. The formula prefix (=) is entered first. If text is included in the formula, the text prefix (") is entered immediately after the formula prefix. In this case, "="In Stock" is entered so that it appears in every record. You then key in the data to be shown in each record.

You can easily change field entries of this kind by using any of the editing methods outlined later in this chapter.

FUNCTIONS

Functions are used in a database to calculate complex formulas based on the contents of fields within that database. A function can also test for conditions and perform specified tasks according to whether the condition is true or false.

You enter functions into the database by first inserting the formula prefix and then the name of the function. Type in a left parenthesis, and then add the names of the fields by typing them in or by pointing to them, followed by a right parenthesis. When you press Enter, Works will calculate the function according to the field entries in individual records.

A function entered in a field in one record appears in the same field in each database record automatically.

Works provides a total of 57 functions, which can be used in both the Database and Spreadsheet tools. A list of some of them is shown in the table in **Chapter 4 — The Spreadsheet.** A complete list can be found in **Appendix B** of the **Microsoft Works User's Guide.**

Figure 21. To enter a function into the database you are creating, highlight the field in which the function is to be located and key in the formula prefix (=). Then type in the condensed name of the function. In this case, "PMT" is used to determine the yearly periodic payment of a loan.

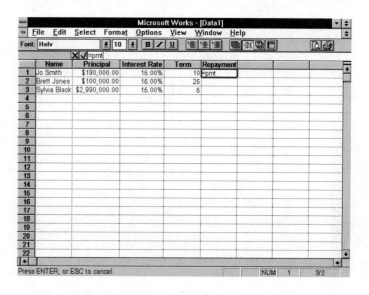

Works bases this calculation on the principal amount borrowed, the rate of interest, and the term over which the loan is required.

Figure 22. The next step is to type a left parenthesis and point to the appropriate fields in the correct order specified by the function. When using the PMT function, point to the "Principal" field first. The current status of the function appears in the Formula Bar. Fields in a function are separated by a comma, so while the "Principal" field is highlighted, key in a comma. The pointer immediately jumps back to the original cell.

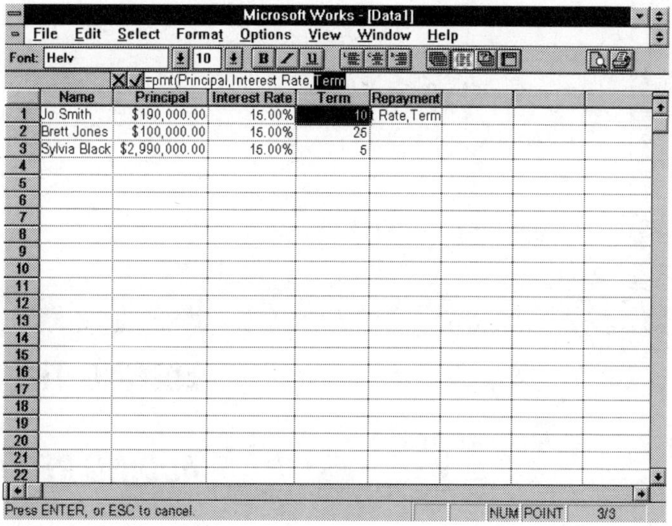

You then point to the "Interest Rate" field and add a comma, and finally the "Term" field. To complete the function, type a right parenthesis and press Enter.

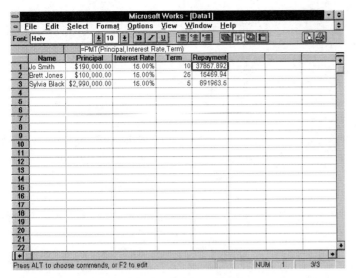

Figure 23. The function will be calculated, showing the result as field entries in every record, and displaying the function in the Formula Bar.

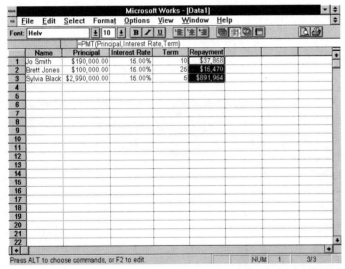

Figure 24. The actual result can be formatted to display in the appropriate numeric format using the options in the **Format** menu.

EDITING THE DATABASE

ADDING RECORDS

One of the advantages of using a computerized database is that it is flexible enough to expand easily. As your company grows, for instance, more and more clients are added to the client list. Adding these extra clients, in database terms, is simply a matter of adding records to the database.

New records can be added to the end of the database, or inserted between current records. Inserting records maintains the order of the records without having to re-sort the database. Records can be added in either List view or Form view.

Figure 25. To add a record in Form view between existing records, move through the database to find the record before which the new record is to be placed. Ctrl+Page Down and Ctrl+Page Up can be used to move to other records. You can use the record number on the Status Bar as a reference if necessary.

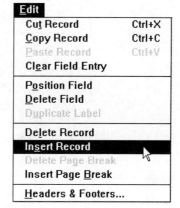

When correctly positioned, choose *Insert Record* from the **Edit** menu. The new record will be inserted immediately. It will be given the record number of the record previously shown on the screen. For instance, if Record 5 was on the screen, the new record becomes Record 5. The original Record 5 becomes Record 6 and the rest of the database is renumbered automatically.

Figure 26. The new record is simply a blank form based on the database structure that has been designed. New field entries can be inserted in exactly the same way as discussed previously.

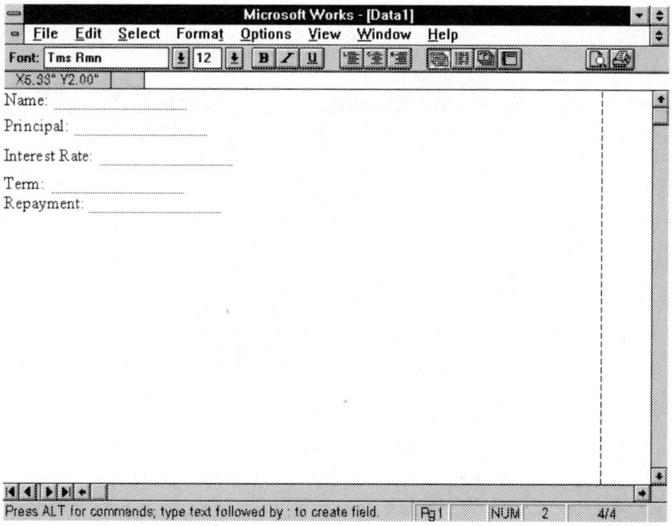

You can insert records between existing records in List view by first highlighting the row where you want the new record to go. To highlight the row, click on the row number in the frame.

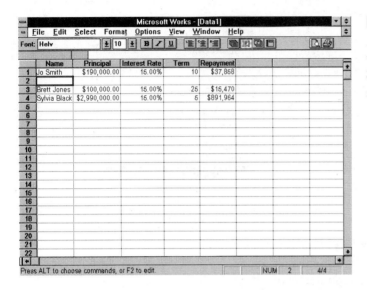

Figure 27. Selecting *Insert Record/ Field* from the **Edit** menu pushes the records in the database down one row and adds a blank record at the highlighted row.

DELETING RECORDS

Updating databases often involves deleting records that are no longer relevant. Records can be deleted in both List and Form views. In both cases, it is important to highlight the record to be deleted.

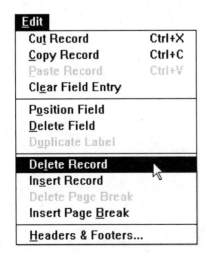

Figure 28. In Form view, Works considers the record that is displayed to be highlighted. (Remember, in Form view, only one record is shown on the screen at a time.) With this in mind, display the record to be removed from the database and choose *Delete Record* from the **Edit** menu.

Figure 29. To remove a record in List view, highlight the record by clicking on the appropriate record number on the frame. Choose *Delete Record/Field* from the **Edit** menu, and the record will be deleted from the database permanently.

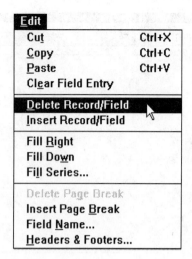

EDITING FIELD NAMES

Once a database has been created, it is necessary to change a name you have given to a field. The field name may need to be replaced with one which is more descriptive or more relevant, or perhaps the original contains a spelling or typing error.

Figure 30. To change a field name in Form view, first highlight the field so that the text appears in the Formula Bar. In this diagram, the field name, Cheese Type, has been highlighted.

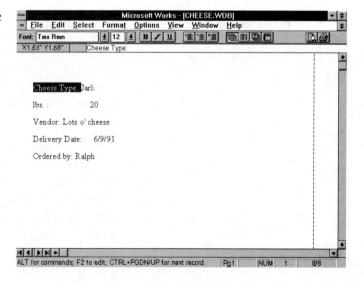

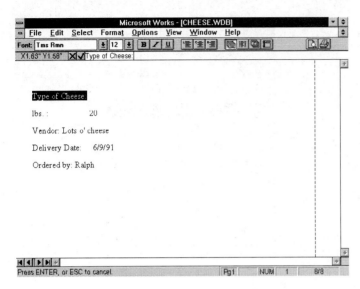

Figure 31. As you type, the new text appears in the Formula Bar. Don't forget to include the colon at the end of the field name.

The field name can also be edited, avoiding the need to retype the data completely. To edit a field entry, the text cursor must be positioned in the Formula Bar. This can be done by clicking the I-beam in the Formula Bar or by pressing F2.

When in the Formula Bar, the text cursor can be moved in the text in much the same way as in a Word Processor document. The Left and Right arrow keys on the keyboard move the text cursor one position in either direction. Pressing Home or End moves the text cursor to the beginning or end of the text, respectively.

Existing text can be added to, changed, and deleted. When you are satisfied with the changes, press Enter. Do not delete the colon when you edit in this way.

Just as it was necessary to add the colon when the field name was entered originally, Works needs to be informed that this is a field name—and not a comment—by typing a colon at the end of the field name when it is retyped. If a colon is not keyed in at the end of a field name, Works will display a warning dialog box.

The dialog box asks you whether the field entries in this field are to be removed. The reason for this question is that you are essentially deleting the field name by not adding the colon. All the data in this field will be lost if you click on *OK*. This could be a very costly mistake, so click on *Cancel* and type in the colon, then press Enter again. The new name becomes part of the database, retaining the original field width.

Figure 32. To change a field name in List view, highlight the field and select the *Field Name* command from the **Edit** menu. In the *Field Name* dialog box, type the new field name into the *Name* text box and click on *OK*.

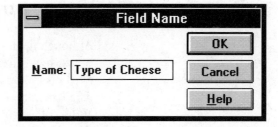

EDITING FIELD ENTRIES

If a field entry contains an error, or just needs to be changed to update a client's personal details, you can make the change by retyping or editing existing text in the Formula Bar.

Figure 33. The field entry to be changed must be highlighted before it can be altered. You can then edit the text by retyping it completely or by adjusting existing text when the text cursor is in the Formula Bar.

If you accidentally delete the text prefix when editing, Works will automatically insert a new prefix.

In a similar fashion, you can also change a field entry in List view.

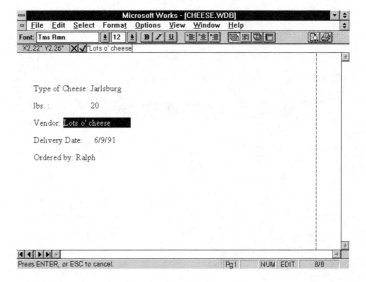

EDITING FIELD SIZES

Although field sizes have no relevance to the amount of text that can be contained in the field, the width of a field is important in the visual display of the database in both Form and List views. In these views, Works offers you a method of widening the field through menu commands as well as a short cut using the mouse.

Changing the field size in Form view will not affect the size of fields in List view, and vice versa.

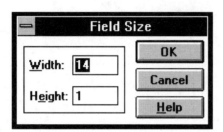

Figure 34. In Form view, the field size is altered using the *Field Size* command in the **Format** menu. When this command is selected, the *Field Size* dialog box appears on the screen. This is identical to the dialog box used to determine the original size of the field. In this dialog box, enter the width and height required, and click on *OK.*

Alternatively, click on a field entry area and a handle will appear in the bottom right corner of the field. You can now resize the field using the mouse by dragging this handle to a new position.

Figure 35. As you drag the handle to the right the field becomes wider. To narrow the field, drag the handle to the left. Increase the height—the number of lines—in the field by dragging the handle down. To display fewer lines in the field, drag the field handle up.

Figure 36. In List view, only the width of the field can be altered. This is done through the menu by choosing the *Field Width* command from the **Format** menu.

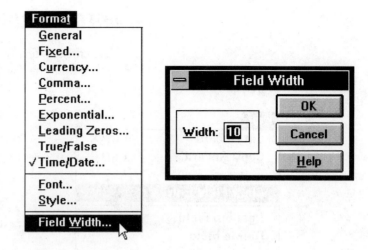

When this command is selected, the *Field Width* dialog box appears, allowing you to key in the new width. Clicking on *OK* changes the width of the entire column in which the pointer is located.

Figure 37 shows how to increase the width of the field using the mouse.

Figure 37. The mouse cursor changes shape when you move it onto the horizontal frame. The width of a field can be adjusted by using this mouse cursor to drag the column border on the frame to the left to make it narrower, or the right to make it wider.

Click and drag the border until the field is the desired width. Release the mouse button and Works will redraw the screen displaying the new field width.

Mouse cursor

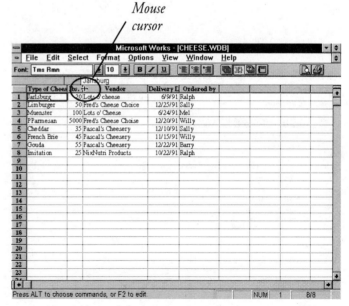

DELETING FIELDS

Field entries—text, values, and formulas—can be deleted from the database using the **Edit** menu or the Delete key.

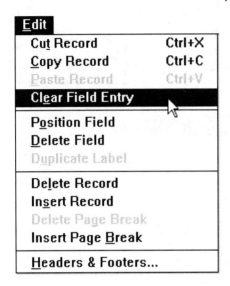

Figure 38. To delete values and text from a field in either view, you must highlight the field first. Then select *Clear Field Entry* from the **Edit** menu and the contents of that field are removed.

The field entry can also be removed by pressing the Delete key when the field is highlighted. This removes the field entry from the Formula Bar only. Should you change your mind, press Esc and the field entry will reappear in the Formula Bar. Pressing Enter after Delete is pressed will remove it from the field entirely.

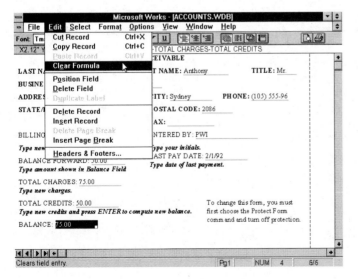

Figure 39. You can delete formula using the *Clear Formula* command in the **Edit** menu. In Form view, simply highlight the field in which the formula is located. In List view, however, you must select the entire field.

Works recognizes that a formula is being removed, changing the *Clear Field Entry* command to *Clear Formula* in the **Edit** menu. Select this command to remove the formula from all entries in that field.

CUTTING, COPYING, AND PASTING

Cutting, Copying, and Pasting follow the same
procedure as in the other Works tools, which were
outlined in **Chapter 2 — Common Features.**

CUTTING, COPYING, AND PASTING FIELDS

Individual field entries can only be Cut, Copied, and
Pasted in List view. The reason for this is that in
Form view, an entire record is displayed—and
therefore highlighted—at any time.

Figure 40. To cut or copy fields in
a database, highlight the field to
be manipulated in List view and
choose the appropriate command
from the **Edit** menu—*Copy*, for
instance.

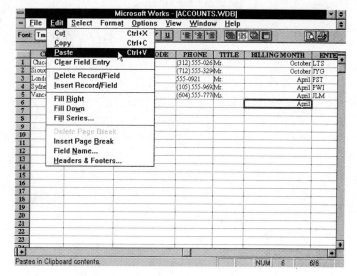

To reinsert the data in the
database, move the pointer to the
correct position and choose *Paste*.

CUTTING, COPYING, AND PASTING RECORDS

An entire record can be cut or copied in either List or
Form view. In Form view, the record displayed on the
screen will be copied or cut. In List view, you must
select the record to be edited by clicking on the record
number on the frame.

Edit

Cu**t** Record	Ctrl+X
Copy Record	Ctrl+C
Paste Record	Ctrl+V
Cl**e**ar Field Entry	
Position Field	
Delete Field	
Duplicate Label	
De**l**ete Record	
In**s**ert Record	
Delete Page Break	
Insert Page **B**reak	
Headers & Footers...	

Figure 41. The *Cut, Copy,* and *Paste* commands from the **Edit** menu in Form view (as shown) are quite different from those in List view (see Figure 40). The Form view commands tell you that only a record can be copied, cut, or pasted.

FILL COMMANDS

As in the spreadsheet tool, the *Fill* commands in the **Edit** menu copy identical information to adjacent cells quickly. This command is available only in List view, where more than one record can be seen. For further information about the *Fill* commands, see **Chapter 4 — The Spreadsheet.**

FORMATTING

Many of the formatting features outlined in this section are common to all Works tools.

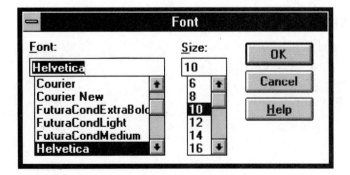

TEXT APPEARANCE

Figure 42. You can alter the appearance of text by using the Toolbar or the *Font* and *Style* commands in the **Format** menu. These latter commands display dialog boxes where you can enter changes to affect the appearance of text in highlighted fields.

When a font and font size is changed in the Database tool, the entire view is affected by the change. Each field in every record will display in the new font. Changes made in Form view do not change the appearance of those in List view, and vice versa.

Figure 43. Styles can be applied to individual fields. These changes remain constant in both List and Form view.

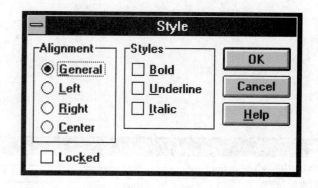

The alignment of fields can also be changed in either List or Form view by selecting one of the alignment options in the *Style* dialog box. Alternatively, click on one of the alignment buttons on the Toolbar. Changes to alignment remain constant in both views.

NUMERIC STYLE

Numeric styles of values and results of formulas can be changed to suitable styles using the **Format** menu. The numeric styles available are identical to those in the Spreadsheet tool. Details on these can be found in **Chapter 4 — The Spreadsheet.**

Numeric formats affect every field in a record. Because of this, you need only select one of the field entries in the field to be formatted. Any changes made in List view change the format of the values in the same field when Form view is displayed, and vice versa.

SORTING

Records in a database can be sorted into alphabetical or numerical order. Up to three fields can be sorted at a time. A three-field sort, for example, is particularly useful when you are sorting a list of names into alphabetical order.

The *1st Field* would sort "Last Name." If more than one person has the same last name, Works would sort those names in alphabetical order based on first name as the 2nd Field. Finally, the 3rd Field would sort the fields based on "Initial."

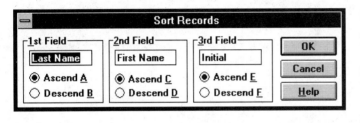

Figure 44. To apply a three-level sort of this kind, choose *Sort Records* from the **Select** menu in either Form or List view. Type the names of the fields into the appropriate text boxes. In this case, "Last Name" is inserted into *1st Field*, "First Name" into *2nd Field*, and "Initial" into *3rd Field*. You would leave the *Ascend* radio button checked to ensure that the names appear in A to Z order and not the reverse.

Click on *OK* to perform the sort. Works reorders the records in the database according to the specifications in the *Sort Records* dialog box.

PROTECTING A FORM

Often a form can take a lot of time to develop to make it look "just right." When you were adding fields to the database in Form view, you learned how easy it was to move fields and comments. However, because this is so easy to do, accidents can occur.

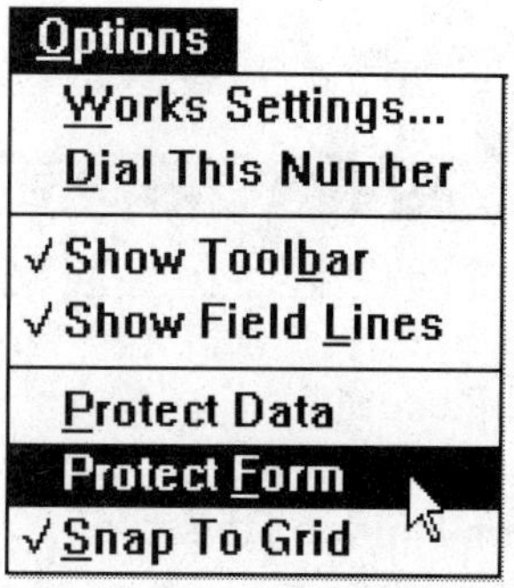

Figure 45. To avoid making accidental changes to the layout of the form, choose *Protect Form* from the **Options** menu. This command, when selected, locks fields and comments into position in the form. Changes can only be made by deselecting the command and then rearranging the data.

Options
Works Settings...
Dial This Number
√ **Show Toolbar**
√ **Show Field Lines**
Protect Data
Protect Form
√ **Snap To Grid**

VIEWING THE DATABASE

KEYBOARD SHORTCUTS

Methods of moving through the database differ between views. The keyboard shortcuts for moving through the database in each view are outlined in the tables illustrated.

Form view Move	Keystroke
Up or down to next field	Up or down arrow
Next/Previous field (unlocked)	Tab/Shift Tab
First/Last record	Ctrl+ Home/End
Next/Previous Record	Ctrl+Page Up/Down

List view Move	Keystroke
First/Last field	Home/End
Next/Previous field (unlocked)	Tab/Shift Tab
First/Last record	Ctrl+ Home/End
Next/Previous Record	Up/Down arrow

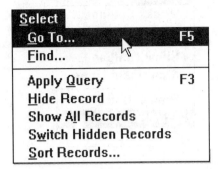

GO TO COMMAND

Figure 46. To move to a specific field or record quickly, use *Go To*. You can activate this command by pressing F5 or by choosing the *Go To* command from the **Select** menu.

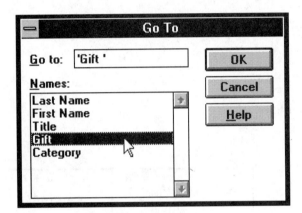

Figure 47. To move to a particular field, you can either type in the name of the field required or select it from the *Names* list box in the *Go To* dialog box. If you want to move a record, type in the number of the record in the *Go to* text box and click on *OK* to move to that field or record.

HIDING DATA

Databases often contain confidential information. Hiding data from public view is therefore an important part of database development.

FIELDS

Fields can be hidden completely only in List view. This is done by adjusting the width of a particular field.

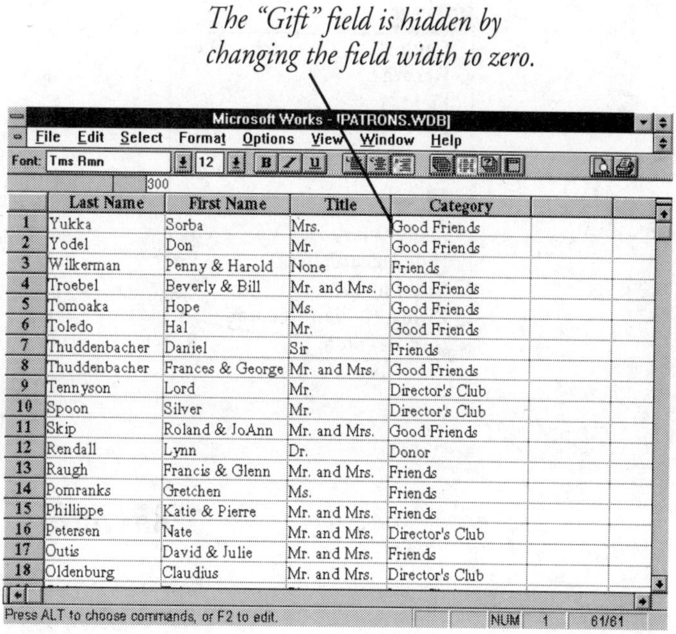

The "Gift" field is hidden by changing the field width to zero.

Figure 48. To hide a field in List view, change the field width to zero using either method covered earlier in this chapter. To redisplay the field, highlight the field using *Go To*. The cursor is placed in the hidden field, where you can change the column width back to the original setting using the *Field Width* command in the **Format** menu.

RECORDS

When you want to hide an entire record from view, first highlight it in either List or Form view.

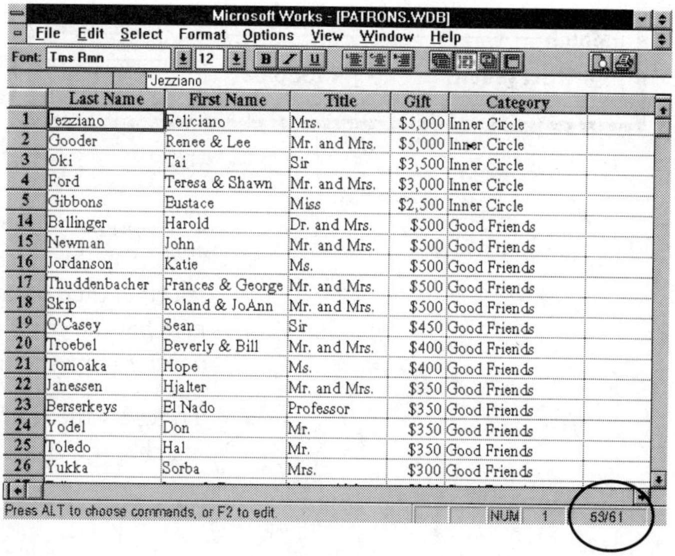

Figure 49. The *Hide Record* command in the **Select** menu allows you to hide records from view. The records remain part of the database, but cannot be seen. Works informs you that not all records are visible in the Status Bar. It will say something similar to "9/10," which tells you that only nine of the ten files in the database are currently displayed.

Figure 50. *Switch Hidden Records* in the **Select** menu operates as a toggle switch between the hidden and nonhidden records. To see just the hidden files, select *Switch Hidden Records* from the **Select** menu. To redisplay the nonhidden files, select the command again.

To redisplay the entire database, select *Show All Records* in the **Select** menu.

SEARCHING

A search is performed in a database to find records that contain specific field information. The first step in performing a search is to select the *Find* command from the **Select** menu.

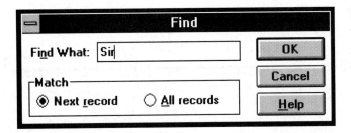

Figure 51. Key in the data for which Works is to search into the *Find What* text box exactly as it appears in the database.

The options in the *Match* group specify how Works is to display the data on the screen. If *Next record* is selected, then the next record in the database that matches the criteria is displayed in Form view—or the pointer moves to it in List view.

To repeat the search—and find the next record that matches the criteria—press F7.

Figure 52. If *All records* is selected, then only those records that match the criteria will be displayed. The number of records matching the criteria is indicated in the Status Bar.

To redisplay the entire database, select *Show All Records* from the **Select** menu.

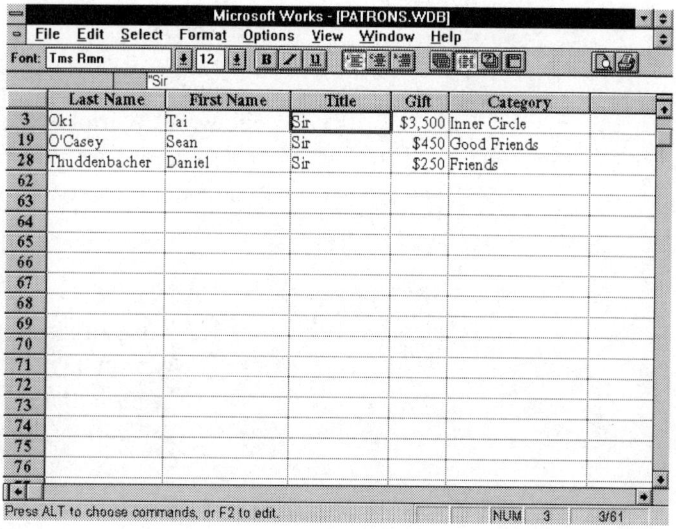

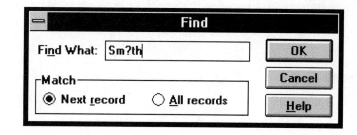

You can use wild card characters to extend the search. The wild cards that can be used are the asterisk (*) and the question mark (?). The asterisk represents any number of characters. For example, key in "555*" to find all the records that contain a phone number starting with 555.

Figure 53. The question mark represents one character. An example of using this wild card could be to find all your clients with the surname of Smith or Smyth. To apply this search, type in "Sm?th" in the *Find What* text box.

145

QUERIES

A query is similar to a search, but much more powerful. Various types of queries can be applied to select records conforming to specific criteria. Some of these options are to search for records that match criteria:

- Exactly
- Based on greater or less than comparisons
- Within a given range
- In more than one field
- By not matching in one or more fields

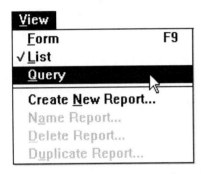

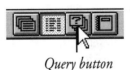

Query button

Figure 54. Queries can be activated only in Query view, which is displayed by selecting *Query* from the **View** menu or by clicking on the *Query* button in the Toolbar.

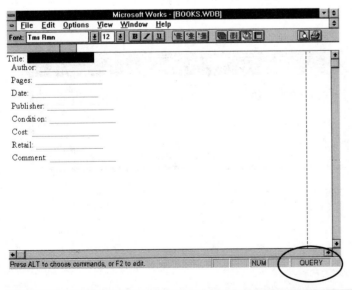

Figure 55. Query view displays an outline of the database. In this outline, only the names of the fields are displayed. As a reminder, QUERY appears in the Status Bar.

Figure 56. Query instructions are typed in the entry area of the appropriate field. To add query instructions, select the field and type in the query instructions. For example, to perform a query based on greater or less than comparisons, type in <200 (and press Enter) to find the books with less than 200 pages.

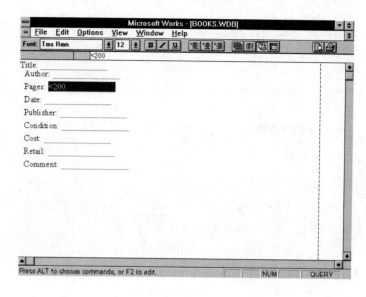

Figure 57. To view the records that match this criteria, switch to List view or Print Preview.

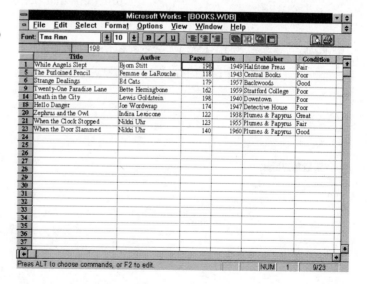

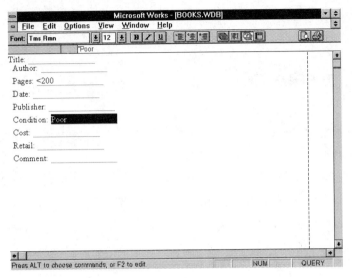

Figure 58. You could apply a more detailed query to the database by adding to this original query. You will have to move back to Query view to do this. In Query view, this time specify—more precisely—which books of less than 200 pages you want to find; for example, those in "Poor" condition.

To perform this query, type "Poor" into the "Condition" field and move back to List view or Print Preview to see the results.

When you have finished with a query, you can clear the query screen by selecting *Delete Query* from the **Edit** menu.

A query can also be based on mathematical instructions. Such instructions can include formulas or functions that perform calculations within a query.

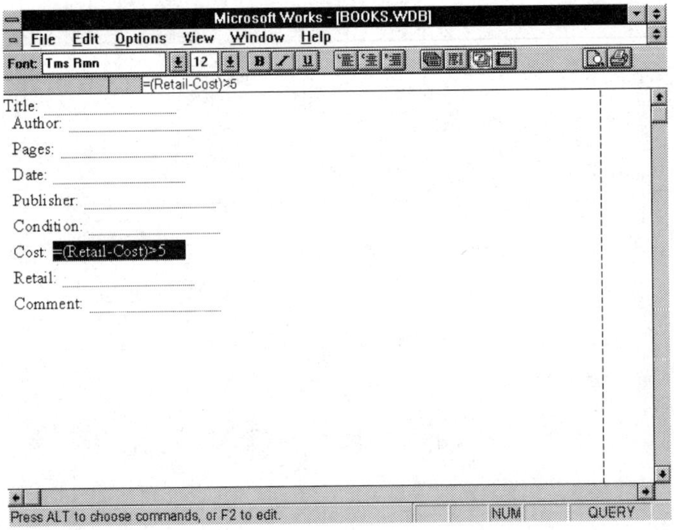

Figure 59. A formula in a query can find records based on the result of a calculation. An example of such a formula could be to find the books that have a mark-up of more than five dollars.

The following formula would be used—"=(Retail-Cost)>5". This formula will calculate the difference between the Retail and Cost prices, determine which records have a result of more than five dollars, and display those records in List view and Print Preview.

REPORTING

Reports are generated in a database to organize and summarize database information. Printing a report gives you much more flexibility than printing straight from List or Form view. When the Report facilities are used, you can:

- Specify fields to print and where they are to appear on the page
- Sort and group fields
- Perform calculations to show statistics about the groups
- Add extra information, such as headings, subheadings, and comments, which add meaning to the report

CREATING A REPORT

Figure 60. A new report can be created by clicking on the *Report* button or selecting *Create New Report* from the **View** menu.

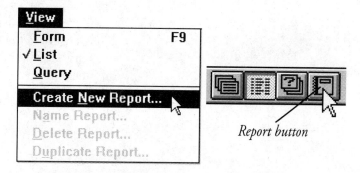

Report button

Figure 61. Works immediately displays the *New Report* dialog box, which allows you to specify the basic structure of the new report. Using this dialog box, you can also enter the report title, which will appear at the top of the page when the report is printed. In this case we entered "Interesting Book Store."

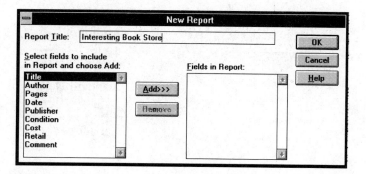

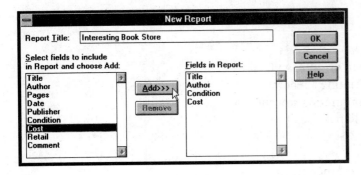

Figure 62. The fields to be included in the report are also specified in the *New Report* dialog box. To add a field to the report, click on the name of the field required in the list box on the left-hand side of the dialog box and then on the *Add* button.

Continue adding the fields using this method until all the fields you want included in the report appear in the *Fields in Report* list box.

To remove a field, click on the unwanted field in the *Fields in Report* list box and then on the *Remove* button.

The next stage in creating a report involves adding report statistics. The *Report Statistics* dialog box (Figure 63) appears automatically when *OK* is clicked in the *New Report* dialog box. This new dialog box adds statistics to the report. Statistics are not essential in a report, but are very useful in summarizing field information.

Seven types of statistics can be applied:

Sum:	adds values in a field
Average:	averages values in a field
Count:	counts the number of entries in a field
Minimum:	finds the lowest value
Maximum:	finds the highest value
Standard Deviation:	calculates the standard deviation of a field
Variance:	calculates the variance of a field

Figure 63. To add statistics, choose the field to which the statistics are to refer from the *Fields in Report* list box. In this case the average cost of the books will be calculated using the settings illustrated.

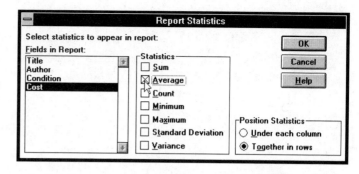

Figure 64. To create the report, click on *OK* in the *Report Statistics* dialog box. When Works has finished creating the report, it displays a dialog box informing you that to see the report as it is printed, you must use *Print Preview*. What is then displayed on the screen is referred to as the *report definition screen*.

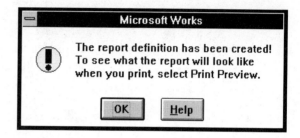

THE REPORT SCREEN

Figure 65. Although the report definition screen uses many of the standard features in Works, it is very different from other screens in the database. The report screen is illustrated here, and its components are described on the following page.

The report definition screen is a grid divided into columns and rows. The columns are labeled with letters and the rows are labelled with various parts of the report. Their order reflects the order in which the report will be printed.

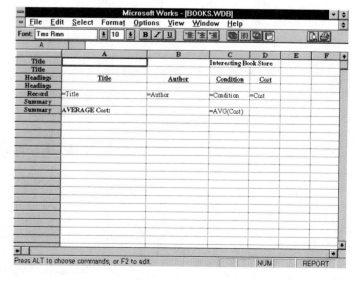

Title			Interesting Book Store	
Title				
Headings	Title	Author	Condition	Cost
Headings				
Record	=Title	=Author	=Condition	=Cost
Summary				
Summary	AVERAGE Cost:		=AVG(Cost)	

Figure 66. The title is printed at the beginning of the report; "Title," therefore, is the first row in the report definition screen. Text in the grid to the right of the title label will be the title that is printed. The title "Interesting Book Store" was inserted in the *New Report* dialog box in Figure 61. It is inserted in column C, which means that it will be printed in the center of the page.

The next two rows contain headings that will appear in the report. This report has four headings, which correspond to the field names inserted into the report—*Title, Author, Condition, Cost.* The second heading row is blank, which means that a blank line will be inserted under the headings to separate them from the fields in the report.

The "Record" row shows which fields will appear in the report when it is printed. In the report definition screen the actual fields are not shown, just the field name with an equals sign (=) prefix. In Print Preview, and when the report is printed, the field entries corresponding to those field names will be inserted into the report.

The "Summary" rows display the formulas used to calculate the statistics. Statistics are calculated in Print Preview and when the report is printed. The result is inserted in place of the formula in the actual report.

MODIFYING A REPORT

The report can be modified in many ways in the report definition screen. When the font or font size is changed, the entire report is affected. The alignment and style of part of the report can be formatted individually. These changes are made using the Toolbar or menu commands outlined in **Chapter 2 — Common Features.**

Figure 67. Text and formulas in the report can be edited by clicking on the "cell" to be modified and making the necessary changes in the Formula Bar. For more details, refer to the editing techniques outlined earlier in this chapter.

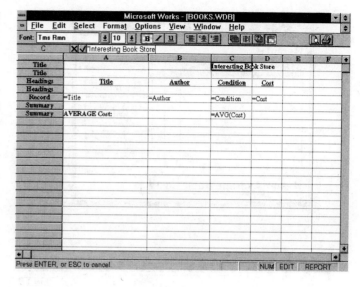

MULTIPLE REPORTS

Numerous reports can be created from the same database file. These reports are automatically named "Report" and given a number according to when they were developed—for example, *Report1*.

Figure 68. Each report included with the database file is listed in the **View** menu. To display one of these files, click on the name of the report in the **View** menu. To redisplay the database in List or Form view, click on either the List or Form view button on the Toolbar, or select one of these commands from the **View** menu.

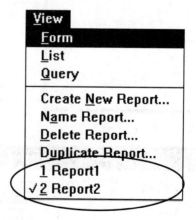

The names "Report1," "Report2," etc., are not descriptive enough to let you know what the report is about. To overcome this problem, you can give the report a name that is more meaningful.

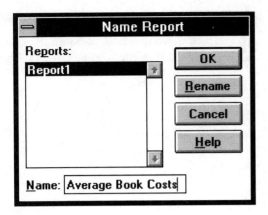

Figure 69. To name a report, select *Name Report* from the **View** menu. In the *Name Report* dialog box, type the new name into the *Name* text box while the correct report is selected in the *Reports* list box. Click on the *Rename* button and then on *OK*. This name change will be reflected in the list of reports in the **View** menu.

PRINTING REPORTS

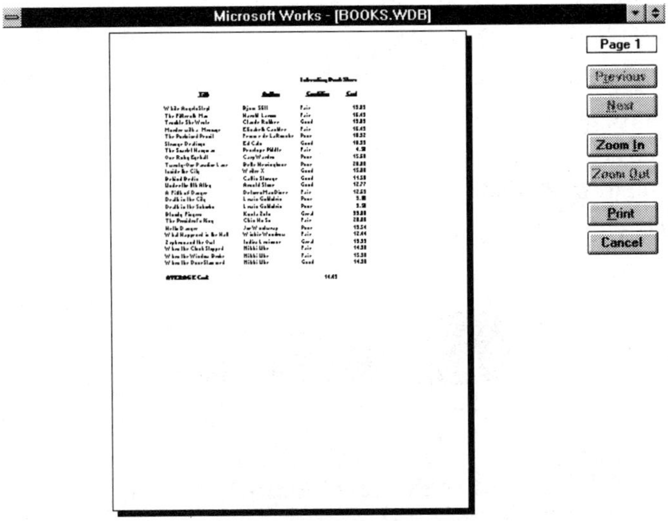

Figure 70. The printed report is quite different from what appears in the report definition screen. Because of this, view the report in *Print Preview* before sending the report to the printer. In order to preview it, display the report in the report definition screen before selecting *Print Preview* from the **File** menu. Alternatively, click on the *Print Preview* button.

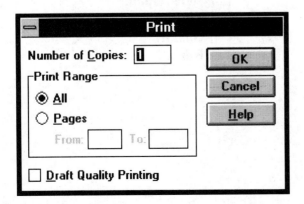

Figure 71. You can print a report directly from *Print Preview* or by selecting *Print* from the **File** menu. The *Print* dialog box appears, allowing you to specify exactly how the report is to be printed. The options include the number of copies, the pages to print, and the quality of the printout.

INTEGRATING THE WORKS TOOLS 6

INTRODUCTION

Works for Windows is an integrated product that combines a number of application types—or tools—into one software package. Works consists of three packages—the Word Processor, the Spreadsheet, and the Database.

Integrating the data created within the separate tools is easy with Works. Works enables you to perform the simple tasks such as copying between files of the same and different types. In addition, you can even perform more complex tasks such as merging database information with a document in a word processor file.

In order to use these features efficiently, you need to understand how to work with multiple files in Works. Multiple file handling is covered in **Chapter 2 — Common Features.** You may want to refer back to that section to refresh your memory before continuing.

WORKSWIZARDS

As stated previously, Works is designed as a piece of software in which the components work together. Works provides you with an extra application called WorksWizards, which is an automated series of templates designed to make integrating data straightforward.

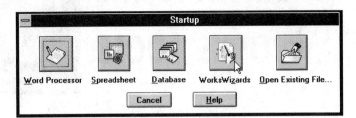

Figure 1. WorksWizards is activated by clicking on the *WorksWizards* button in the *Startup* dialog box. Alternatively, click on the *WorksWizards* button in the *Create New File* dialog box.

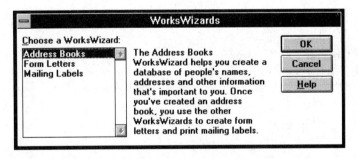

Figure 2. When WorksWizards is started, the *WorksWizards* dialog box appears. In this dialog box you can choose which type of WorksWizard you want to create. There are three types of documents:

1. *Address Book*
2 *Form Letters*
3. *Mailing Labels*

When you have selected the type of document you want to create, click on *OK*. The WorksWizards will guide you through a series of screen displays instructing you how to create the type of file you need.

ADDRESS BOOK

Figure 3. A WorksWizards address book is a database file that contains names and addresses of friends, clients, or any other significant group. The Address Book WorksWizard steps you through the process of creating such a database file.

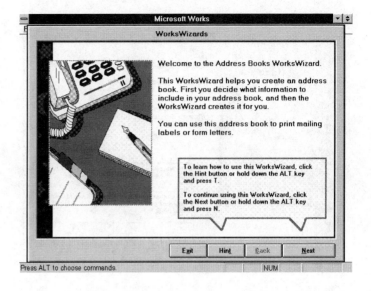

FORM LETTERS

Figure 4. A form letter in WorksWizards is a standard document that is to be sent to the people who are part of the address book. Naturally, you must create the address book before the form letter. Using the Form Letter WorksWizard, you can merge data from the address book into the form letter by following a series of on-screen instructions.

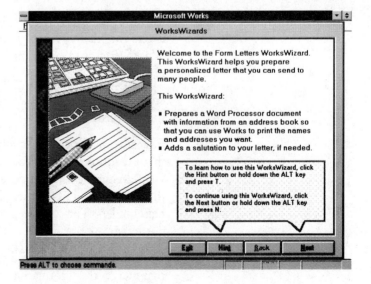

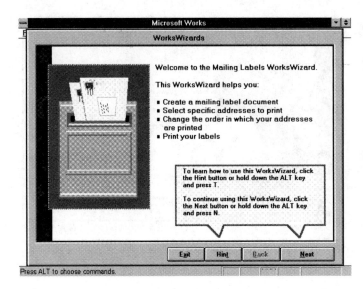

MAILING LABELS

Figure 5. When the letters are printed and ready to be mailed, you can invoke the Mailing Label WorksWizard to prepare the labels for the envelopes. Once again, data from the address book is used in the mailing labels—another example of integrating data with the WorksWizards.

INTEGRATING DATABASE INFORMATION WITH THE WORD PROCESSOR

Works Wizards are useful for integrating data to create form letters and mailing labels. However, it is not essential to invoke WorksWizards to create these documents.

The procedures outlined in this section will enable you to create form letters and mailing labels without having to call on the "Wizards."

Basically, the procedure involves creating a database document that is equivalent to the Address Book in WorksWizards. Then you develop the form letter, in which you refer to the fields in the database and insert them into the document as placeholders. The same steps are followed for the mailing labels document.

Finally, the form letters and mailing labels are printed in a way that merges the information in both the word processor file and the database file. The following pages cover these procedures in detail.

THE DATABASE FILE

Figure 6. The first step is to create an appropriate database file. This file could include fields of this kind: First Name, Last Name, Address (which contains the street number and street), Suburb, City, Zip Code, Country, and any other items that are relevant.

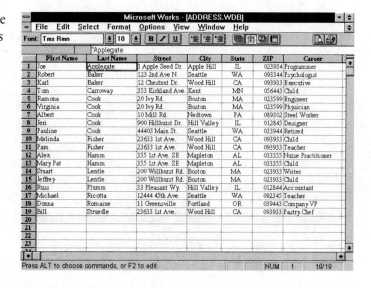

When you are creating a file of this kind, it is better to break the database into the smallest possible fields. For example, do not make "First Name" and "Last Name" one field called "Name."

Combining these fields is not useful because you would lose flexibility. For example, if the database were sorted based on the last name of a person, Works would be unable to access the first letter of the last name if it were part of the overall field of "Name."

The database file can contain fields that will not be included in the form letter or mailing labels. Any fields that are not included in the form letter or mailing label documents are ignored when the files are merged.

THE FORM LETTER DOCUMENT

The form letter is created in a new Word Processor document, which is opened by selecting *Create New File* from the **File** menu, or by clicking on the *Word Processor* button in the *Startup* dialog box.

When creating the form letter document, you must also open the database file with which the form letter is being merged.

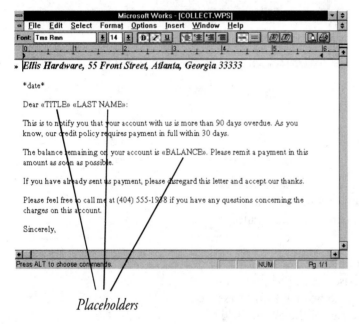

Placeholders

Figure 7. This figure shows a completed form letter similar to the one that you will be shown how to create in the following pages. As you can see, a form letter document contains a combination of text and database fields. The text makes up the bulk of the letter.

The database fields are represented in the form letter as "placeholders," which are simply the names of the fields enclosed by chevrons (<< >>). These are not typed in, but are inserted in a special way outlined in this chapter so that Works can replace the field "placeholder" with field entries from the database file when the form letter is printed.

Figure 8. Field placeholders must be inserted into the document with the *Database Field* command in the **Insert** menu. Before selecting this command, place the text cursor in the precise position you want the placeholder to go. In this figure, the company logo is inserted first, and the text cursor is positioned ready for the first placeholder—<<First Name>>.

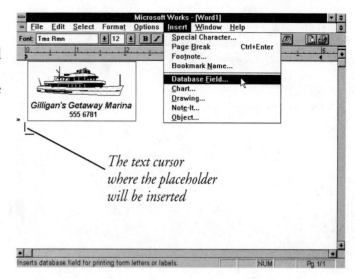

The text cursor where the placeholder will be inserted

Figure 9. Selecting the *Database Field* command displays the *Insert Field* dialog box. This allows you to determine the database with which the form letter will merge, as well as the actual fields being inserted. All of the database files that are currently open are listed in the *Databases* list box.

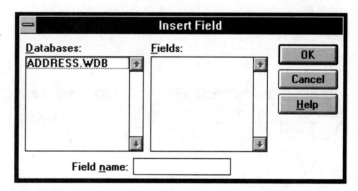

Figure 10. To obtain a list of fields, select the database file name you want to use from the *Databases* list box. All of the fields within that database will appear in the *Fields* list box. Once the field names are listed, click on the field you want inserted into the form letter at the cursor position, and then on *OK*.

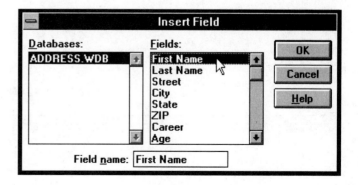

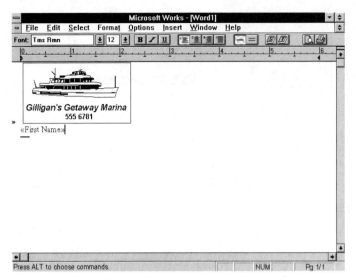

Figure 11. The field name becomes part of the document. It is enclosed by chevrons (<< >>), which indicate that it is in fact a field name placeholder, not just normal text. If the chevrons are deleted accidentally, reinsert the field in the same way as outlined above. Typing the field name and the chevrons from the keyboard will not perform the merge correctly.

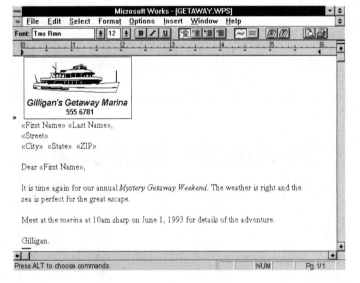

Figure 12. Continue creating the form letter using the text required, as well as inserting the field names using the *Database Field* command in the **Insert** menu.

When the document is complete, save the file. We have named ours *getaway.wps*.

PRINTING A FORM LETTER

Form letters are not printed using the standard *Print* command in the **File** menu. This command prints simple documents that do not require merging. If this command were activated, the form letter would be printed exactly as it appears on the screen. *Print* cannot insert field entries into the placeholders.

Figure 13. The command used to print form letters is *Print Form Letters* in the **File** menu. The database file, with which the form letter file is being merged, must be open before this command is selected. In the *Print Form Letters* dialog box, click on the database file required in the *Databases* list box.

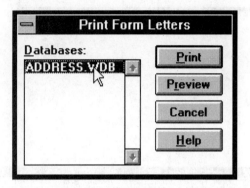

Page 6 displays the information from record 6 in the database merged into the form letter.

Figure 14. The *Preview* button in the *Print Form Letters* dialog box is used to view the form letters before they are printed. Use this command to check that the fields are inserted in the correct place before sending them to the printer.

When in *Print Preview*, you will notice that Works has created a new form letter for each record in the database. Each letter will be printed on a new page.

Click on the *Print* button to return to the *Print Form Letters* dialog box.

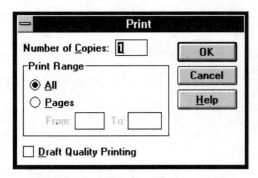

Figure 15. The form letters are printed by clicking on the *Print* button in the *Print Form Letters* dialog box (Figure 13). The *Print* dialog box appears, which is standard to all Works tools. It can be used to specify the number of copies, print range, and quality of printing. Click on *OK* to send the form letters to the printer.

THE MAILING LABEL DOCUMENT

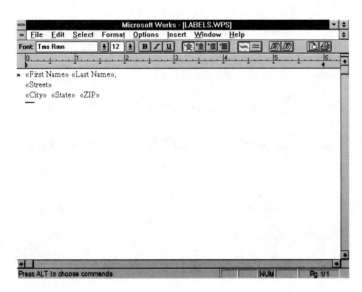

Figure 16. A mailing label document is also created with the *Database Field* command in the **Insert** menu, in the same way as a form letter. The major difference is that the document should only contain relevant information for mailing labels— names and addresses.

A sample mailing label document is shown in this figure.

The information in the label document will be used as the structure for each of the mailing labels.

PRINTING MAILING LABELS

Figure 17. Mailing labels must be printed with the *Print Labels* command in the **File** menu. This command must be used for the same reason that form letters are printed with the *Print Form Letters* command—Works cannot merge files using the standard *Print* command.

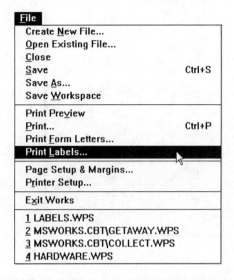

Figure 18. In the *Print Labels* dialog box, you need to specify the database being used in the *Databases* list box. Once again, this list box lists only the database files that are open.

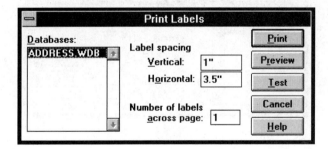

The dialog box allows you to specify the label dimensions that are being used. These specifications depend on the actual label pages being fed through the printer.

The *Vertical* label spacing specifies the distance from the top of one label to the top of the label underneath. The *Horizontal* label spacing measures from the right of one label to the right of the other.

The *Number of labels across page* text box determines the number of labels that fit across the page—that is, how many columns of labels there are.

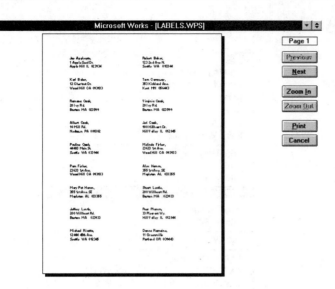

Figure 19. You can check the layout of the labels on the screen using the *Preview* button in Figure 18. Click on *Print* to return to the *Print Labels* dialog box.

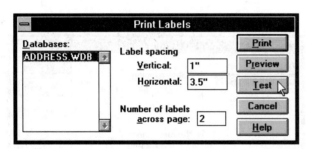

Figure 20. The *Test* button in the *Print Labels* dialog box will print the first two rows of labels to the printer to check the final output. This is a more economical approach than sending the entire file.

Figure 21. To print all the labels, click on *Print.* Clicking on this button displays the *Page Setup & Margins* dialog box, which can be used to make any final changes to the label page structure.

For example, the labels you have specified may not fit between the margins. If you try to print without adjusting the margins, the dialog box shown above will appear. If it does appear, change the margins and try again!

Figure 22. The next dialog box to appear is the standard *Print* dialog box. Click on *Print* to send the labels to the printer.

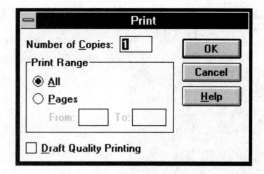

INTEGRATING SPREADSHEET INFORMATION WITH THE WORD PROCESSOR

Spreadsheet information is often required in a Word Processor document. For instance, spreadsheet data may be needed in monthly and annual reports, or in quotes and tenders. These are usually presented in a written document, which requires the spreadsheet data in particular places in the document.

Integrating spreadsheet data into a Word Processor file saves you time in rekeying figures and eliminates the risk of error.

Spreadsheet data can be inserted into a Word Processor file using worksheet cells, or as a chart based on the spreadsheet information.

IMPORTING WORKSHEET DATA

Worksheet cells are imported into the Word Processor as a table in columns and rows. This information usually contains calculations, but can be text only. Text-only tables can eliminate the need to create a table using tabs and borders within the Word Processor.

To import worksheet data, both the Spreadsheet and Word Processor files must be created and open.

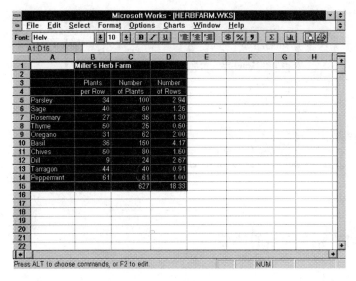

Figure 23. The worksheet data will be placed in the Word Processor document at the cursor position, so position the cursor correctly before proceeding. Then move into the Spreadsheet window and highlight the worksheet cells required in the Word Processor document. Copy these cells in the normal way.

When the cells are copied, move back to the Word Processor through the **Window** menu.

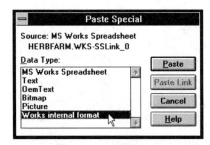

Figure 24. The *Paste Special* command in the Word Processor **Edit** menu is more powerful for copying between tools than the standard *Paste* command. The *Paste Special* dialog box allows you to specify the type of import Works is to perform.

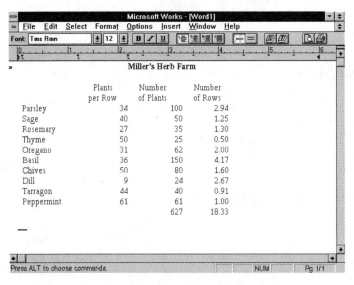

A standard import places the worksheet data in the Word Processor document in a table—using a tab delimiter—to separate the cell entries. To perform this standard type of import, keep *Works internal format* selected as the *Data Type* in the *Paste Special* dialog box and click on *Paste*.

LINKING THE SPREADSHEET DATA

A standard import pastes the data into the document as text only. No reference is made by Works to its origin. It is often useful, however, to record this information and create a dynamic link back to the original source in the Spreadsheet file.

A link ensures that the worksheet data in the Word Processor will be automatically updated whenever you make a change to the worksheet. It also allows you to easily move back to the Spreadsheet file.

Figure 25. To create a link, choose *MS Works Spreadsheet* as the *Data Type* in the *Paste Special* dialog box after the worksheet data has been copied and you have returned to the Word Processor. When this option is selected, the *Paste Link* button becomes active. Click on this button to import the data, thus creating a link between the worksheet and the Word Processor document.

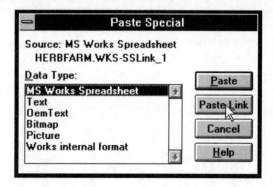

Figure 26. When the *Paste Link* method is used, the worksheet data is placed in the Word Processor document as a table whose cells are separated by gridlines.

To return to the worksheet, double-click on the table. When you are back in the worksheet, you can make any necessary changes. They will be reflected back in the Word Processor document automatically.

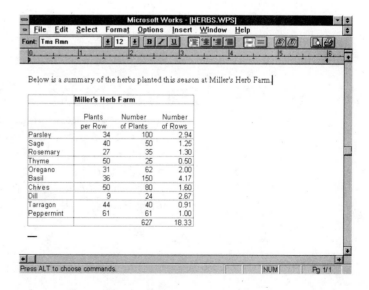

IMPORTING A CHART

To import a chart into a Word Processor document, first copy the chart onto the clipboard. The chart is copied by displaying it on the screen and selecting *Copy* from the **Edit** menu.

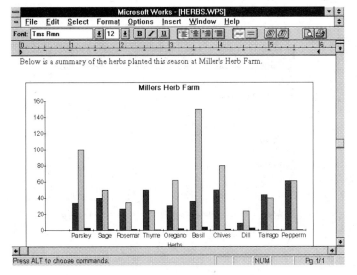

Figure 27. The chart is imported into the Word Processor document using the *Paste Special* command in the **Edit** menu. When a chart is on the clipboard and the *Paste Special* command is selected, Works selects the *Data Type* as *MS Works Chart* by default. Click on the *Paste Link* button to insert the chart into the Word Processor document, which automatically creates a link back to the chart in the Spreadsheet file.

The chart can be updated easily by double-clicking on the chart in the Word Processor document, or by clicking once on the chart and selecting *Edit Chart Object* in the **Edit** menu. Either of these options opens the Spreadsheet file in which the chart is located and displays the chart on the screen. Any changes made to the chart, including formatting, will update the chart in the Word Processor file.

BREAKING A LINK

If the link becomes redundant, you can break it using the *Links* command in the **Edit** menu. This command is available only when a linked object is selected.

Figure 28. A list of the linked objects in a document is provided in the *Links* dialog box. To break the link, ensure that the correct object is selected, then click on *Cancel Link*.

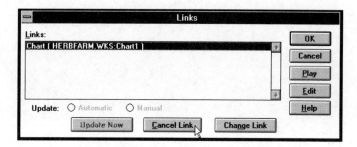

When you return to the document by pressing *OK*, the link is broken. The chart or worksheet information will no longer update automatically.

The other options in this dialog box are outlined below.

Update	is used to change the type of link from *Automatic* to *Manual* and vice versa.
Update Now	will update the linked information when the update mode is *Manual*.
Change Link	is used to change the link between the linked information and the file to which it is connected.
Cancel Link	cancels the link to the original document.
Play	starts the linked application.
Edit	starts the linked application so that the document can be edited.

DIALOG BOXES

LOCATING DIALOG BOXES

The following pages provide a visual summary of how to access Works dialog boxes.

COMMON DIALOG BOXES

Some dialog boxes common to the modules—Startup, Works Settings and the **File** menu are shown here.

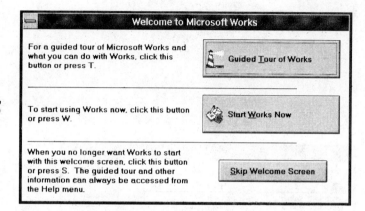

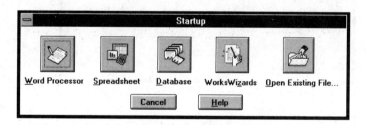

OPTIONS MENU

Options
Works Settings...

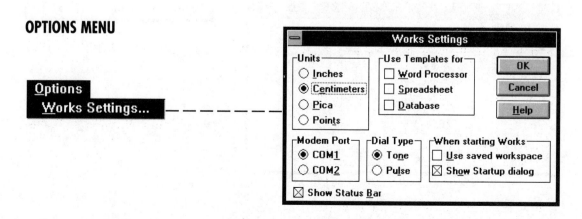

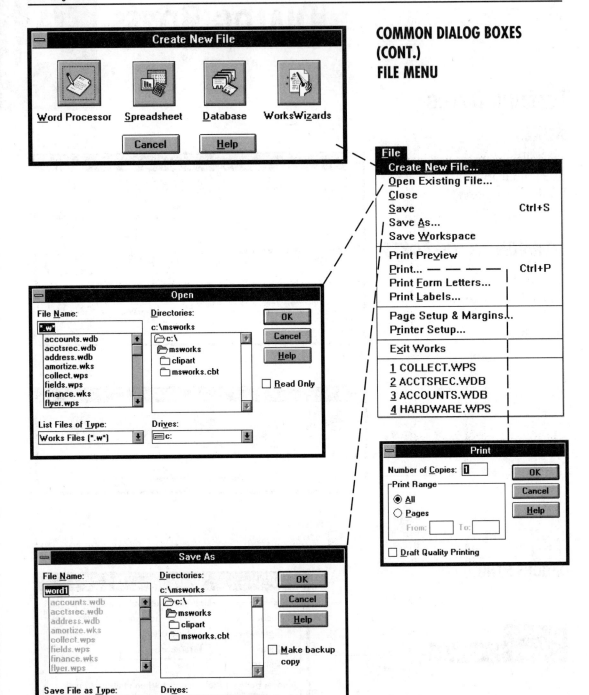

COMMON DIALOG BOXES
(CONT.)
FILE MENU

FILE MENU (CONT.)

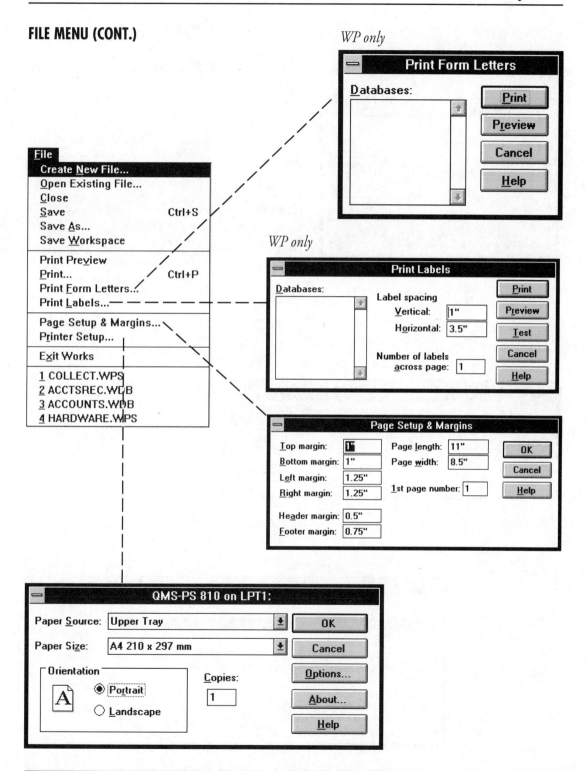

WP only

Print Form Letters

Databases:

Print
Preview
Cancel
Help

File
Create New File...
Open Existing File...
Close
Save   Ctrl+S
Save As...
Save Workspace

Print Preview
Print...   Ctrl+P
Print Form Letters...
Print Labels...

Page Setup & Margins...
Printer Setup...

Exit Works

1 COLLECT.WPS
2 ACCTSREC.WDB
3 ACCOUNTS.WDB
4 HARDWARE.WPS

WP only

Print Labels

Databases:

Label spacing
Vertical: 1"
Horizontal: 3.5"

Number of labels
across page: 1

Print
Preview
Test
Cancel
Help

Page Setup & Margins

Top margin: 1"
Bottom margin: 1"
Left margin: 1.25"
Right margin: 1.25"

Header margin: 0.5"
Footer margin: 0.75"

Page length: 11"
Page width: 8.5"

1st page number: 1

OK
Cancel
Help

QMS-PS 810 on LPT1:

Paper Source: Upper Tray
Paper Size: A4 210 x 297 mm

Orientation
A
● Portrait
○ Landscape

Copies:
1

OK
Cancel
Options...
About...
Help

WORD PROCESSOR

EDIT MENU

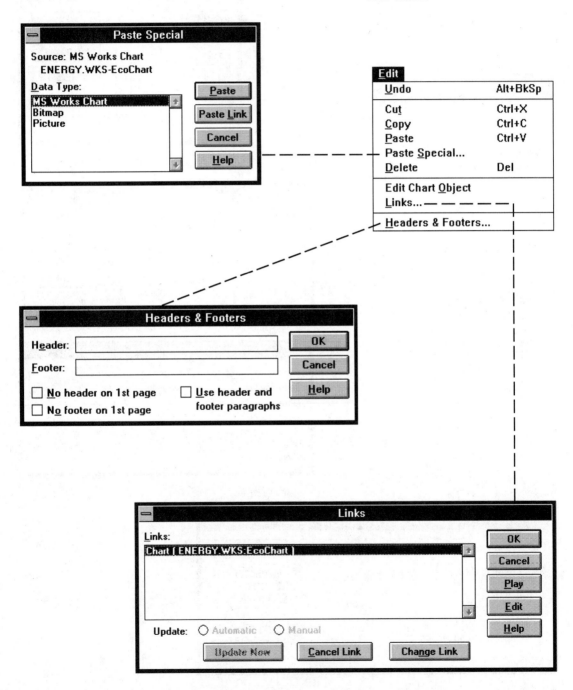

WORD PROCESSOR

SELECT MENU

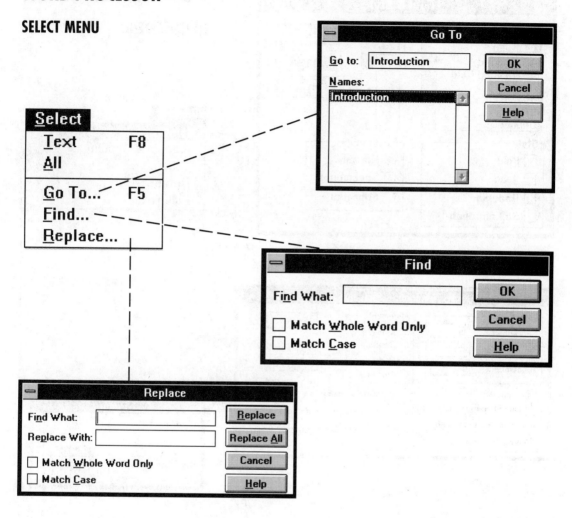

Select

Text	F8
All	
Go To...	F5
Find...	
Replace...	

Go To

Go to: Introduction

Names:
Introduction

OK
Cancel
Help

Find

Find What:

☐ Match Whole Word Only
☐ Match Case

OK
Cancel
Help

Replace

Find What:
Replace With:

☐ Match Whole Word Only
☐ Match Case

Replace
Replace All
Cancel
Help

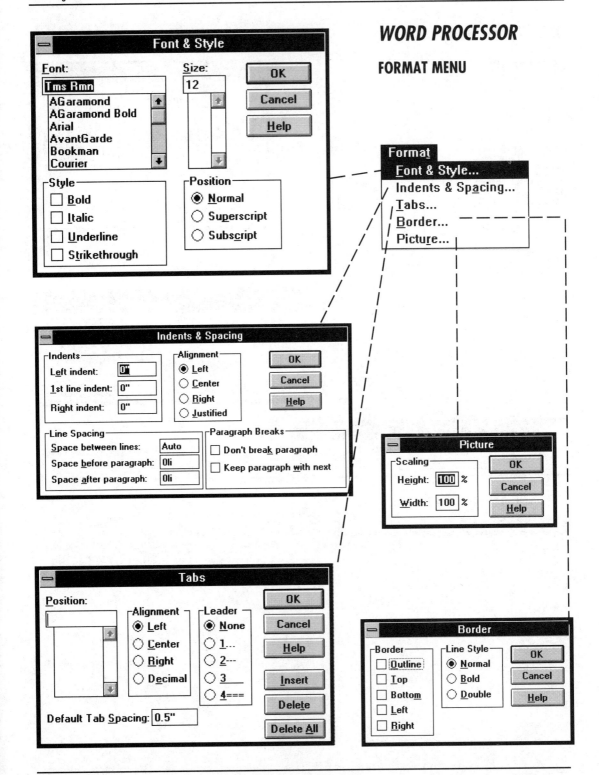

WORD PROCESSOR

FORMAT MENU

Font & Style

Font:
Tms Rmn
AGaramond
AGaramond Bold
Arial
AvantGarde
Bookman
Courier

Size:
12

OK
Cancel
Help

Style
☐ Bold
☐ Italic
☐ Underline
☐ Strikethrough

Position
◉ Normal
○ Superscript
○ Subscript

Format
Font & Style...
Indents & Spacing...
Tabs...
Border...
Picture...

Indents & Spacing

Indents
Left indent: 0"
1st line indent: 0"
Right indent: 0"

Alignment
◉ Left
○ Center
○ Right
○ Justified

OK
Cancel
Help

Line Spacing
Space between lines: Auto
Space before paragraph: 0li
Space after paragraph: 0li

Paragraph Breaks
☐ Don't break paragraph
☐ Keep paragraph with next

Picture

Scaling
Height: 100 %
Width: 100 %

OK
Cancel
Help

Tabs

Position:

Alignment
◉ Left
○ Center
○ Right
○ Decimal

Leader
◉ None
○ 1...
○ 2---
○ 3
○ 4===

OK
Cancel
Help
Insert
Delete
Delete All

Default Tab Spacing: 0.5"

Border

Border
☐ Outline
☐ Top
☐ Bottom
☐ Left
☐ Right

Line Style
◉ Normal
○ Bold
○ Double

OK
Cancel
Help

WORD PROCESSOR

OPTIONS MENU

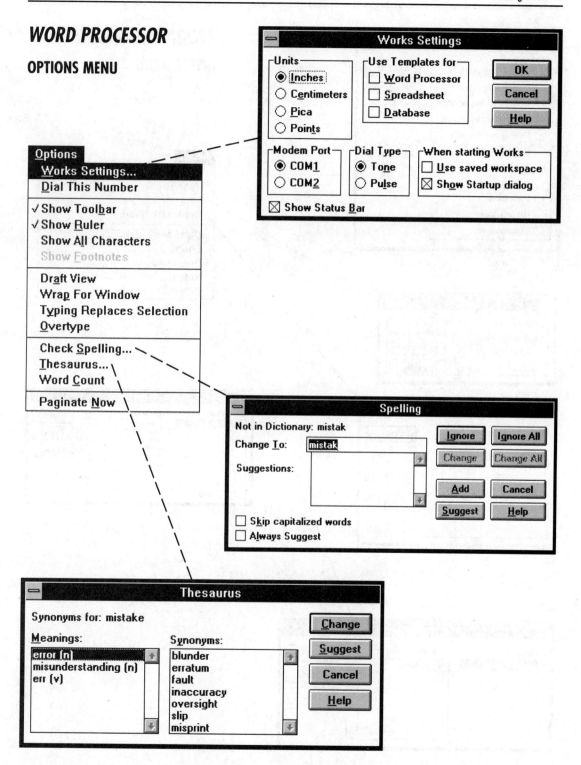

Works Settings

Units
- ⦿ Inches
- ○ Centimeters
- ○ Pica
- ○ Points

Use Templates for
- ☐ Word Processor
- ☐ Spreadsheet
- ☐ Database

OK
Cancel
Help

Modem Port
- ⦿ COM1
- ○ COM2

Dial Type
- ⦿ Tone
- ○ Pulse

When starting Works
- ☐ Use saved workspace
- ☒ Show Startup dialog

☒ Show Status Bar

Options

Works Settings...
Dial This Number

√ Show Toolbar
√ Show Ruler
Show All Characters
Show Footnotes

Draft View
Wrap For Window
Typing Replaces Selection
Overtype

Check Spelling...
Thesaurus...
Word Count

Paginate Now

Spelling

Not in Dictionary: mistak
Change To: [mistak]
Suggestions:

Ignore   Ignore All
Change   Change All

Add   Cancel
Suggest   Help

☐ Skip capitalized words
☐ Always Suggest

Thesaurus

Synonyms for: mistake

Meanings:
- error (n)
- misunderstanding (n)
- err (v)

Synonyms:
- blunder
- erratum
- fault
- inaccuracy
- oversight
- slip
- misprint

Change
Suggest
Cancel
Help

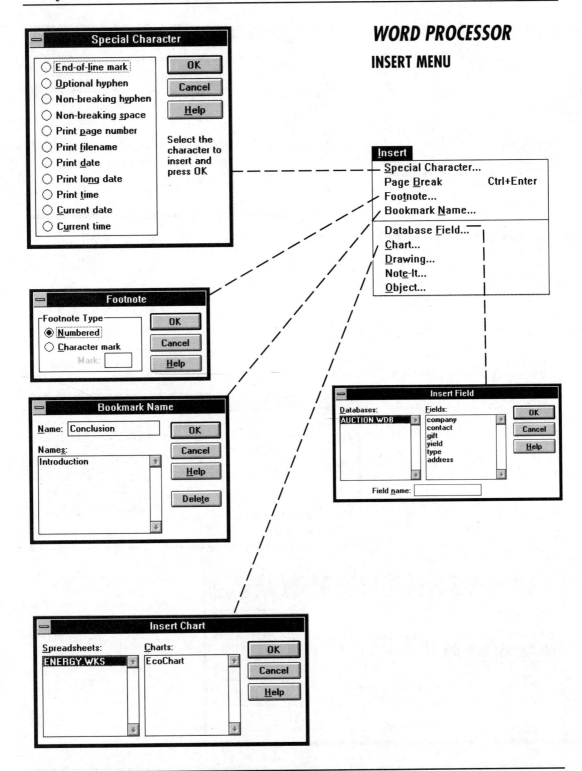

WORD PROCESSOR

INSERT MENU

WORD PROCESSOR

INSERT MENU (CONT.)

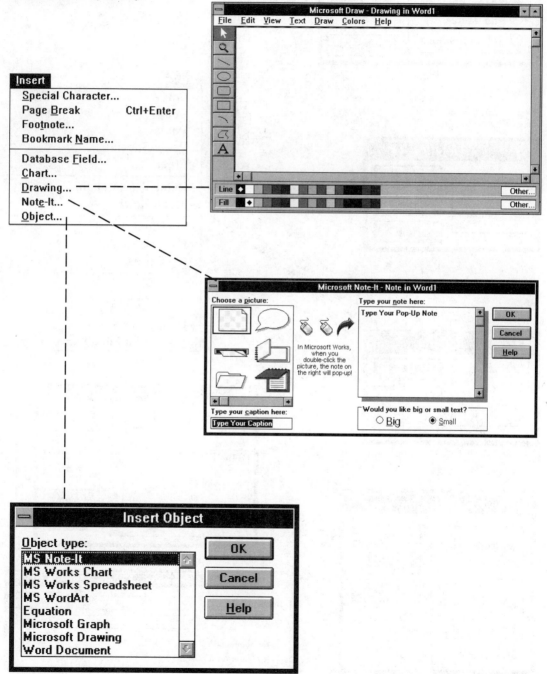

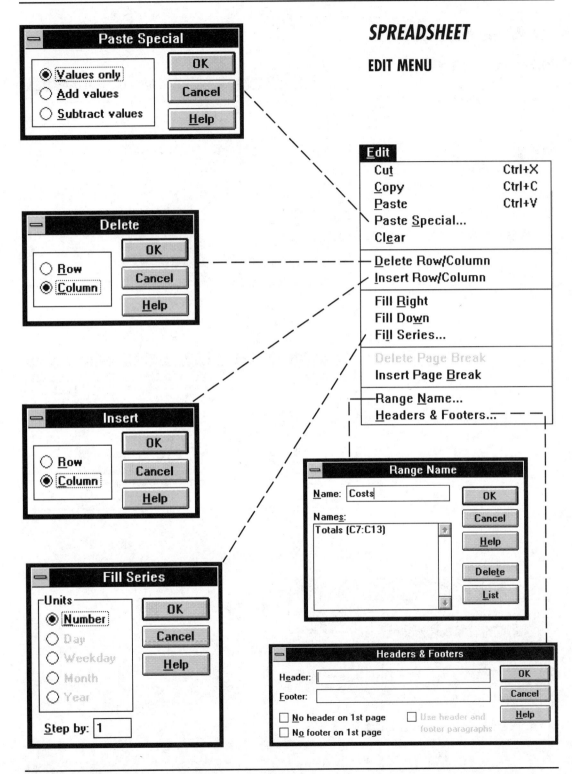

SPREADSHEET

EDIT MENU

Paste Special

- ● Values only
- ○ Add values
- ○ Subtract values

OK
Cancel
Help

Delete

- ○ Row
- ● Column

OK
Cancel
Help

Insert

- ○ Row
- ● Column

OK
Cancel
Help

Fill Series

Units
- ● Number
- ○ Day
- ○ Weekday
- ○ Month
- ○ Year

Step by: 1

OK
Cancel
Help

Edit

Cut	Ctrl+X
Copy	Ctrl+C
Paste	Ctrl+V
Paste Special...	
Clear	
Delete Row/Column	
Insert Row/Column	
Fill Right	
Fill Down	
Fill Series...	
Delete Page Break	
Insert Page Break	
Range Name...	
Headers & Footers...	

Range Name

Name: Costs

Names:
Totals (C7:C13)

OK
Cancel
Help
Delete
List

Headers & Footers

Header:
Footer:

- ☐ No header on 1st page
- ☐ No footer on 1st page
- ☐ Use header and footer paragraphs

OK
Cancel
Help

SPREADSHEET

SELECT MENU

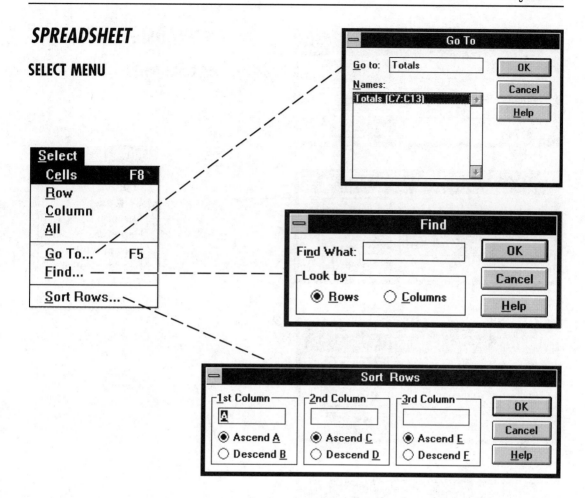

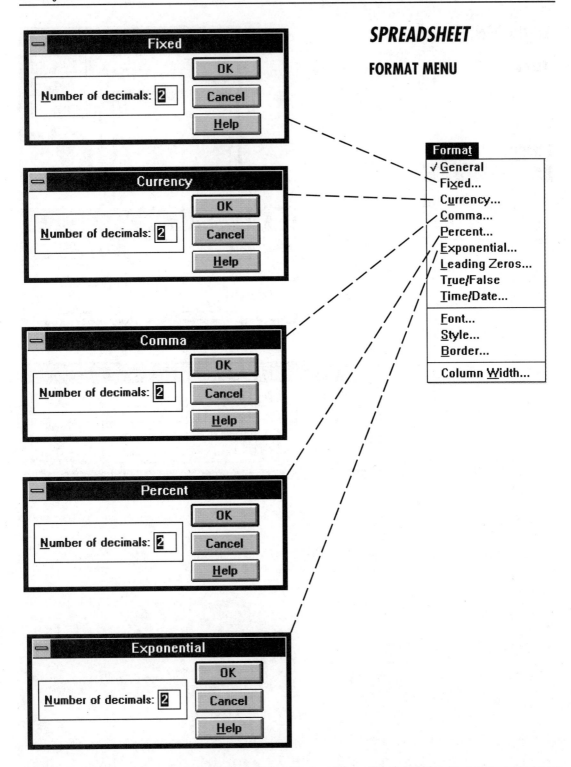

SPREADSHEET

FORMAT MENU

SPREADSHEET

FORMAT MENU (CONT.)

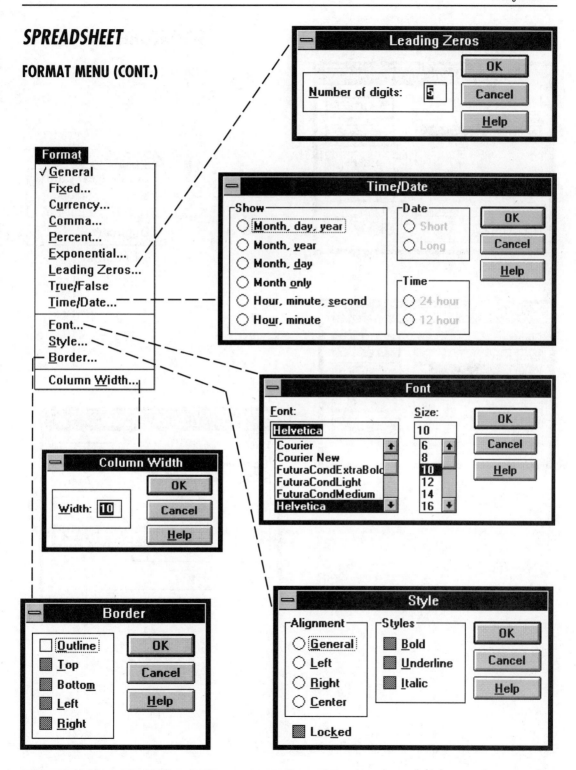

Leading Zeros

Number of digits: 5

OK
Cancel
Help

Format

√ General
Fixed...
Currency...
Comma...
Percent...
Exponential...
Leading Zeros...
True/False
Time/Date...
Font...
Style...
Border...
Column Width...

Time/Date

Show
○ Month, day, year
○ Month, year
○ Month, day
○ Month only
○ Hour, minute, second
○ Hour, minute

Date
○ Short
○ Long

Time
○ 24 hour
○ 12 hour

OK
Cancel
Help

Font

Font:
Helvetica
Courier
Courier New
FuturaCondExtraBold
FuturaCondLight
FuturaCondMedium
Helvetica

Size:
10
6
8
10
12
14
16

OK
Cancel
Help

Column Width

Width: 10

OK
Cancel
Help

Border

☐ Outline
▨ Top
▨ Bottom
▨ Left
▨ Right

OK
Cancel
Help

Style

Alignment
○ General
○ Left
○ Right
○ Center

▨ Locked

Styles
▨ Bold
▨ Underline
▨ Italic

OK
Cancel
Help

SPREADSHEET

CHARTS MENU

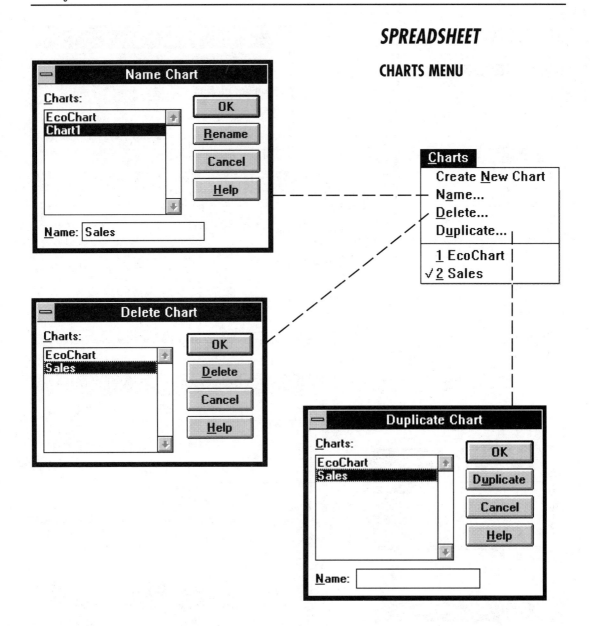

DATABASE

EDIT MENU

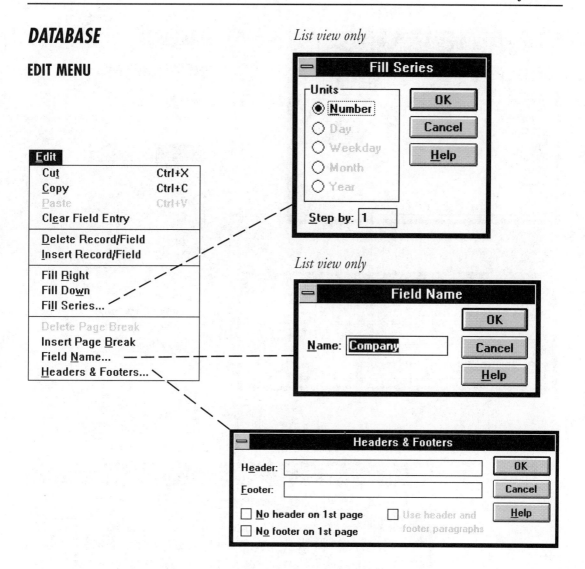

List view only

Fill Series

─Units─
- ⦿ **Number**
- ○ Day
- ○ Weekday
- ○ Month
- ○ Year

OK

Cancel

Help

S̲tep by: 1

Edit

Cut	Ctrl+X
Copy	Ctrl+C
Paste	Ctrl+V
Cl̲ear Field Entry	
D̲elete Record/Field	
I̲nsert Record/Field	
Fill R̲ight	
Fill Do̲wn	
Fi̲ll Series...	
Delete Page Break	
Insert Page B̲reak	
Field N̲ame...	
H̲eaders & Footers...	

List view only

Field Name

OK

N̲ame: Company

Cancel

Help

Headers & Footers

H̲eader: [   ]

F̲ooter: [   ]

- ☐ N̲o header on 1st page
- ☐ N̲o footer on 1st page
- ☐ Use header and footer paragraphs

OK

Cancel

Help

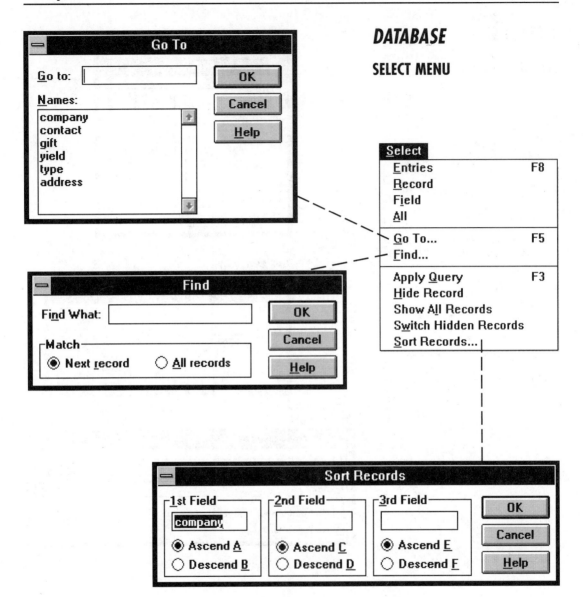

DATABASE

SELECT MENU

Go To

Go to:

Names:
company
contact
gift
yield
type
address

OK
Cancel
Help

Select	
Entries	F8
Record	
Field	
All	
Go To...	F5
Find...	
Apply Query	F3
Hide Record	
Show All Records	
Switch Hidden Records	
Sort Records...	

Find

Find What:

┌Match─────────────────────┐
◉ Next record   ○ All records

OK
Cancel
Help

Sort Records

┌1st Field──┐
company
◉ Ascend A
○ Descend B

┌2nd Field──┐
◉ Ascend C
○ Descend D

┌3rd Field──┐
◉ Ascend E
○ Descend F

OK
Cancel
Help

DATABASE

FORMAT MENU

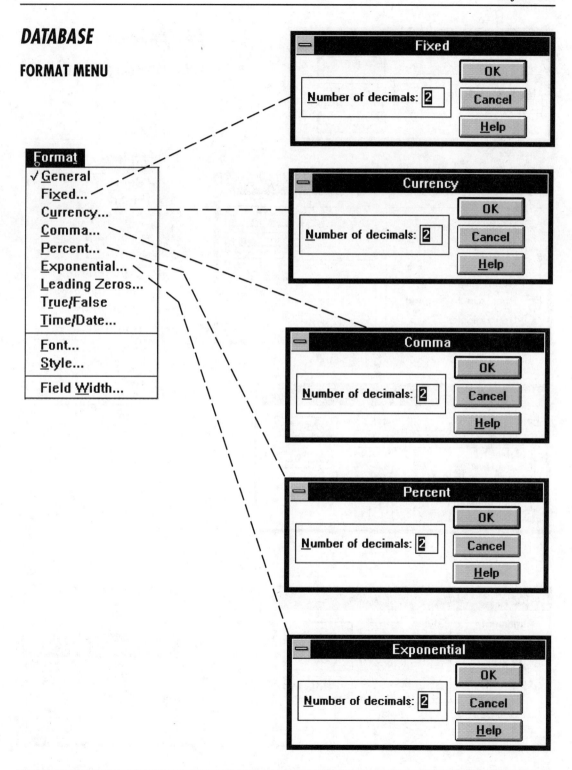

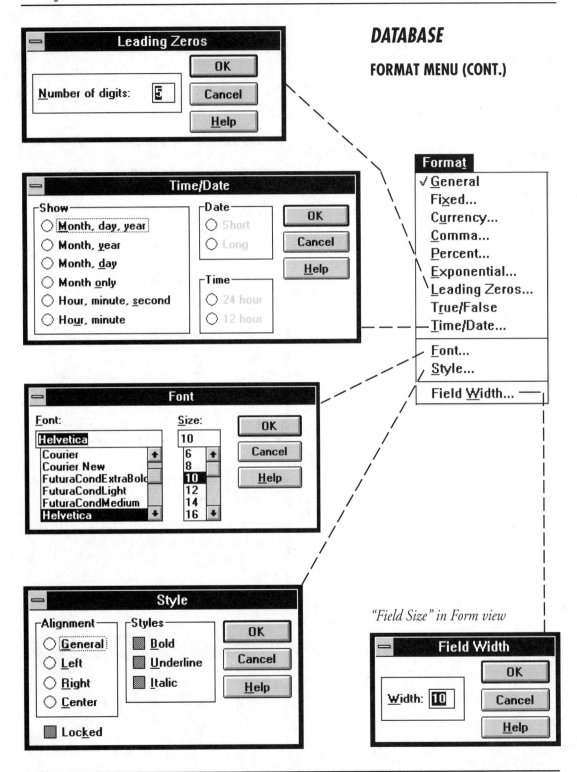

DATABASE

FORMAT MENU (CONT.)

Leading Zeros

Number of digits: 5

OK
Cancel
Help

Format
√ General
Fixed...
Currency...
Comma...
Percent...
Exponential...
Leading Zeros...
True/False
Time/Date...
Font...
Style...
Field Width...

Time/Date

Show
○ Month, day, year
○ Month, year
○ Month, day
○ Month only
○ Hour, minute, second
○ Hour, minute

Date
○ Short
○ Long

Time
○ 24 hour
○ 12 hour

OK
Cancel
Help

Font

Font:
Helvetica
Courier
Courier New
FuturaCondExtraBold
FuturaCondLight
FuturaCondMedium
Helvetica

Size:
10
6
8
10
12
14
16

OK
Cancel
Help

Style

Alignment
○ General
○ Left
○ Right
○ Center

Styles
▓ Bold
▓ Underline
▓ Italic

OK
Cancel
Help

▓ Locked

"Field Size" in Form view

Field Width

Width: 10

OK
Cancel
Help

DATABASE

VIEW MENU

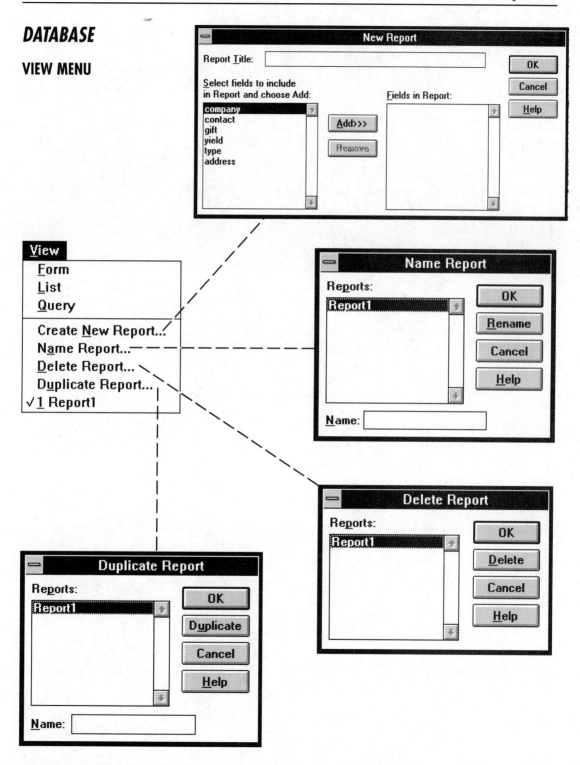

Index